W9-DDU-610

3 1205 0026 2774

WITHDRAWN

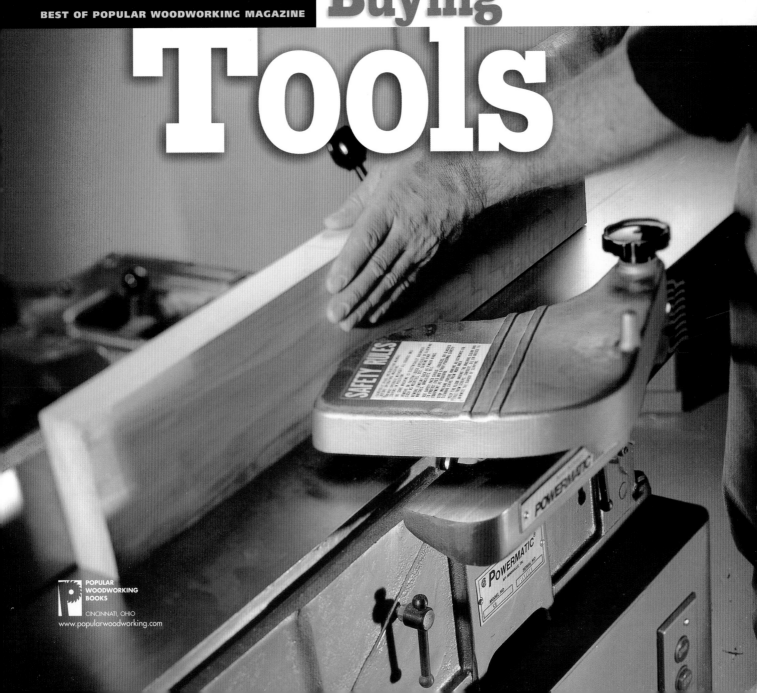

The Insider's Guide to
Buying
Tools

BEST OF POPULAR WOODWORKING MAGAZINE

POPULAR
WOODWORKING
BOOKS

CINCINNATI, OHIO
www.popularwoodworking.com

READ THIS IMPORTANT SAFETY NOTICE

To prevent accidents, keep safety in mind while you work. Use the safety guards installed on power equipment; they are for your protection. When working on power equipment, keep fingers away from saw blades, wear safety goggles to prevent injuries from flying wood chips and sawdust, wear headphones to protect your hearing, and consider installing a dust vacuum to reduce the amount of airborne sawdust in your woodshop. Don't wear loose clothing, such as neckties or shirts with loose sleeves, or jewelry, such as rings, necklaces or bracelets, when working on power equipment. Tie back long hair to prevent it from getting caught in your equipment. People who are sensitive to certain chemicals should check the chemical content of any product before using it. The authors and editors who compiled this book have tried to make the contents as accurate and correct as possible. Plans, illustrations, photographs and text have been carefully checked. Tool prices listed in this book are subject to change based on market fluctuation, manufacturers or other factors. Due to the variability of local conditions, construction materials, skill levels, etc., neither the authors nor Popular Woodworking Books assumes any responsibility for any accidents, injuries, damages or other losses incurred resulting from the material presented in this book.

METRIC CONVERSION CHART

to convert	to	multiply by
Inches	Centimeters	2.54
Centimeters	Inches	0.4
Feet	Centimeters	30.5
Centimeters	Feet	0.03
Yards	Meters	0.9
Meters	Yards	1.1
Sq. Inches	Sq. Centimeters	6.45
Sq. Centimeters	Sq. Inches	0.16
Sq. Feet	Sq. Meters	0.09
Sq. Meters	Sq. Feet	10.8
Sq. Yards	Sq. Meters	0.8
Sq. Meters	Sq. Yards	1.2
Pounds	Kilograms	0.45
Kilograms	Pounds	2.2
Ounces	Grams	28.4
Grams	Ounces	0.04

The Insider's Guide to Buying Tools. Copyright © 2000 by Popular Woodworking Books. Manufactured in China. All rights reserved. No part of this book may be reproduced in any form or by any electronic or mechanical means including information storage and retrieval systems without permission in writing from the publisher, except by a reviewer, who may quote brief passages in a review. Published by Popular Woodworking Books, an imprint of F&W Publications, Inc., 1507 Dana Avenue, Cincinnati, Ohio, 45207. First edition.

Visit our Web site at www.popularwoodworking.com for information about more resources for woodworkers.

Other fine Popular Woodworking Books are available from your local bookstore or direct from the publisher.

04   03   02   01   00   5   4   3   2   1

Library of Congress Cataloging-in-Publication Data

The insider's guide to buying tools / by the editors of Popular Woodworking Books.
    p. cm.
    ISBN 1-55870-542-2 (alk. paper)
    1. Woodworking tools--Purchasing. I. Popular Woodworking Books (Firm).
TT186 .I57 2000
684'.08--dc21   00-036306

Text by Charlie Self and David Thiel
Edited by Jennifer Churchill
Content edited by Michael Berger, Mark Thompson
Designed by Brian Roeth
Production coordinated by Kristen Heller
Copyediting by Diane F. Weiner
Proofreading by Kenya McCullum
Indexing by Brian Feil
Page layout by Donna Cozatchy
Action photography by Al Parrish

84.08
INS
cop.l

Introduction

Welcome to *Popular Woodworking* magazine's *Insider's Guide to Buying Tools*. This book is exactly what the title says it is — your shopping guide for woodworking power tools. Think of it as that next-door neighbor who knows everything about power tools.

When you decide to buy a table saw, go to this knowledgeable "neighbor" for advice. When you go to the store, take your neighbor along with you. He's not just there to tell you what tool to buy — he wants you to understand why you're buying a particular tool, and what makes that tool the right choice for you. He'll point out the features that you should be paying attention to, and explain some of the jargon that can make tool shopping a challenge. Your neighbor will guide you through your purchase, recommend accessories and make sure you don't buy more than you need. And, in the process, he's going to teach you something about tools — so maybe during the next shopping trip, *you* can be the wise neighbor.

But maybe the tool you want to buy isn't available at the local home-center store. Where else can you shop? Your neighbor is here to introduce you to the joys of catalog and Internet shopping — and he'll also warn you about the pitfalls. And when you can't find what you want for the right price, he'll give you some advice on how to shop for the best deal on used power tools.

While shopping for tools is a joy all by itself, there is a lot to learn. To keep your educational trip lively, your neighbor also will take you over to the section of the store where the tools are so

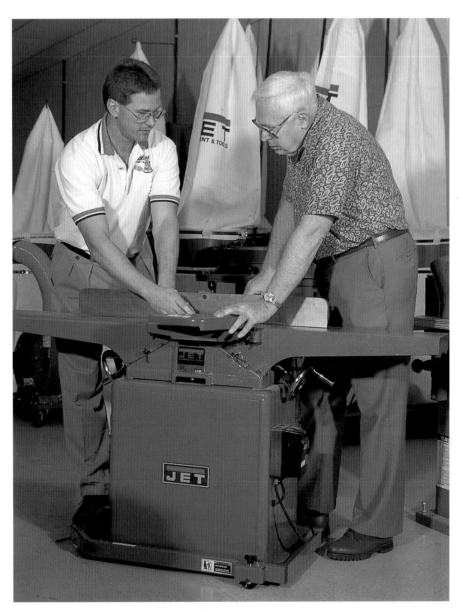

expensive and outrageous that you know you're not going to buy anything. But it's great fun to look and dream — and maybe someday, who knows ...

So sit down and have a chat with your *Popular Woodworking* neighbor

and get some of your most important questions out of the way. Then head for the store! We'll make sure you have the information you need to make a smart decision when you buy your next woodworking power tool.

PUBLIC LIBRARY
DANVILLE, ILLINOIS

Table of Contents

TOOLS

How to Use This Book

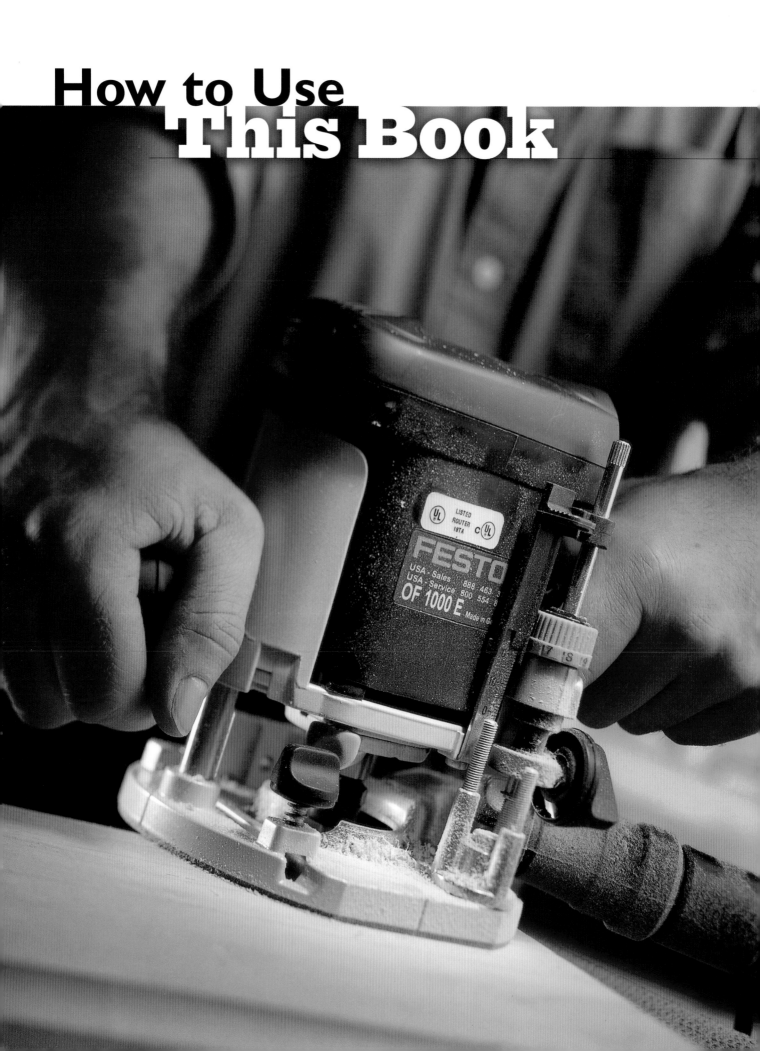

This book is your guide to shopping for woodworking power tools. There are sections covering 15 major tool categories — ranging from rotary tools to table saws. Some of the 15 categories are broken into subgroups to make it easier to find the information of specific interest to you. Each of the tool sections will include a description of what the tool is used for, the features that differentiate one tool from another, what to look for while you're still in the store and other information to help make you an informed tool buyer. We'll also tell you the right questions to ask and other uses for a particular tool, as well as suggest things you can buy to make the tool more versatile.

We've also added information about some non-tool items. Check out the sections "What You Must Know About Motors" and "Choosing the Best Router Bit."

While this book is designed to give you the information you need to make your own decision about which tools are best for you, we know that even after all your research, sometimes it just comes down to a coin toss. We've included a section in each tool chapter that breaks the decision-making process into fast, decision-making advice. And if there is a clear "leader" in a tool category,

we'll tell you what brand or tool that is.

This book is not a catalog list of every tool available. That information changes too rapidly to ever stay current in book form. For that type of listing we suggest any number of woodworking magazines (including *Popular Woodworking*) for current tool information. Another current informational source in this very fluid market is the Internet. We've listed the World Wide Web sites for every major tool manufacturer at the back of the book. These sites will offer very complete lists of tools available from each manufacturer, as well as great detail about each tool's specifications. The manufacturers' sites won't give you prices — so we've also listed some sites for tool shopping.

But learning about tools doesn't have to be all statistics and voltages. We've added some fun in our "All It Takes Is Money" chapter. We went shopping for the cream of the crop in all the tool categories and put together a fantasy shop worthy of Bill Gates' checkbook (assuming he might be a woodworker). We didn't even try to justify why these tools are so expensive — we just went nuts. Hope you have as much fun reading about that fantasy as we had dreaming it up.

What You Must Know
About Motors

Learn to shop smart so you get the right motor for the way you work

By Christopher Schwarz
Christopher Schwarz is senior editor at *Popular Woodworking* magazine

If you're an electrical engineer, you can stop reading this section right now. This information isn't for the gear heads — it's for the rest of you woodworkers who use power tools every day but are occasionally stupefied by amps, volts, watts and horsepower. I'll warn you, there's just the tiniest bit of math to learn here. But if you can multiply and divide two numbers, you will open up a whole new world of understanding when it comes to the subject of motors.

The first thing to understand is that there are two kinds of motors that power almost all of the machinery in a home workshop: induction motors and universal motors. Each type has its strengths and weaknesses. The reason that you need to know the difference between the two is that some tools (table saws, planers and jointers, for example) can be powered by either type of motor. So you need to educate yourself so you'll choose the right motor for the kind of work you do.

In general, induction motors power stationary machinery that must run for hours on end, such as big table saws, planers, band saws and jointers. Universal motors power mostly handheld stuff: routers, jigsaws and sanders. However, this is changing. These days, you'll find more and more universal motors in benchtop table saws and portable planers.

We like to think of the two motors as the tortoise and the hare.

Induction motors are the tortoise of the pair. They're rugged, quiet, large, heavy, turn more slowly and can be stalled under heavy use. They are great for the long haul.

Universal motors, on the other hand, have a shorter life span, they're smaller, they make more noise, they operate at very high speeds, they offer the most horsepower per pound of any alternating current motor, and they are very difficult to stall. Universal motors provide large amounts of power in quick bursts with constant torque and at variable speeds.

It might help to think about how you use tools with universal motors. If you've got a chop saw, you need a burst of power for three or four seconds to make your cut. You need torque and you need it fast. Same goes for biscuit joiners and routers. Unless you are running parts for 100 doors on your router table, chances are that these tools are on for five minutes and then off for a while. Now think about how you use a jointer or a planer with a hefty induction motor. You might have 100 board feet of lumber to surface. Each board might have to go through that machine five times. Your machine might be running for hours on end.

So each type of motor has a type of job that it's really good at. And it all has to do with the way that the motor is built. Here's the inside story:

Induction Motors

The reason they are called "induction" motors is because of the way they convert electricity into a spinning rotor. To understand how induction motors work, let's say you've got one of these puppies in your table saw and you're about to turn it on. As you flip the switch, power flows into what's called the "stator" and magnetizes it. The stator is a mass of copper windings that surround the rotor in the center, which is what spins the saw's blade through a series of belts and pulleys. Inside the stator are two or four "poles" that become magnetically charged because of the electricity running through the wires. When the electricity changes direction or cycles, as it does 60 times a second in the U.S. (hence the term 60 cycles), each pole changes its magnetic strength, from a positive to a negative value or from a negative to a positive value.

The induced poles in the rotor are then attracted and repulsed by these ever-changing electromagnets in the surrounding stator. The motor isn't running, but the rotor is excited. What this hulk of iron and copper now needs is a shot of power from another copper winding (called a "starting winding") that is out of phase physically and electrically with the main winding. And that's where the capacitor comes in. In most modern tools a capacitor (which is in series with the starting winding) helps with the starting torque. Then, when the motor reaches 85 percent of its speed, the capacitor and the starting winding drop out of the circuit and the motor runs on its main winding.

Whew. So, this is the long way to explain why these are called induction motors. As you can see, the rotor spins because it is "induced" by the electromagnets in the stator. Induction motors are large and heavy because the induction process takes a lot of iron and copper (a ½-horsepower induction motor weighs about 25 pounds; a ½-hp universal motor weighs 2½ pounds). Induction motors are reliable because they're simple, their parts are built for long life and they run at slow speeds (so they don't generate as much motor-damaging heat). In fact, a well-built induction motor won't heat up more than 40 degrees centigrade over room temperature. Induction motors are slow because the rotations per minute (rpm) are governed by how many poles are inside the stator and the number of times per second that your electricity cycles — which is standard at 60 cycles. So now you can understand why you wouldn't want your router powered by an induction motor — you could barely lift it, and it probably would be too slow and not have enough torque.

Universal Motors

Universal motors get their name from the fact that many of them can operate on both alternating current (from an outlet) or direct current. The way that universal motors work is a little more complicated than their induction cousins, but there are similarities.

Instead of a rotor, universal motors have what's called an armature that spins in the center. Instead of a stator,

the induction motor

END CAP • Holds the rotor in place inside the stator.

ROTOR • Spins freely inside the stator. Its magnets are attracted and repulsed by the magnets in the stator.

CAPACITOR Gives the rotor the boost it needs at startup.

STATOR • Current magnetizes the copper poles inside.

universal motors have what's called a field, usually consisting of two coils surrounding the armature.

Universal motors also have some parts that induction motors don't. On one end of the armature is a part called the commutator. This part is round like the armature, but it is usually smaller in diameter and is made of small bars of copper. It's through these bars that the armature winding is energized. Universal motors also have what are called "brushes." Brushes are made from a carbon-graphite material and are usually held in place against the commutator by small springs. When you turn on a universal motor, current travels in what's called a "series circuit." One side of the electrical line goes through the field, then through the brushes, into the commutator, then the armature, and back to the other side of the line. Each of the bars in the commutator changes polarity as it contacts a brush, and this changes the polarity in the magnets in the armature. The magnetic forces in the armature react with the electromagnets in the field coils and the motor develops torque.

Universal motors make a lot of noise because they spin at a dizzying speed — sometimes seven times faster than an induction motor — and their fans suck a lot of air through the motor, which makes noise.

Universal motors are less reliable than induction motors for three reasons. First, the motor generates more heat, which can cause the components to break down. Second, the carbon brushes wear out. If they can be replaced, then it's a quick fix. If they can't, you've got trouble. And third, the big fan that cools the motor brings in a lot of junk such as sawdust and foreign objects. This junk can damage the windings and their insulation.

Learn to Shop

Now that you know the differences between induction and universal motors, you need to know how to compare motors when tool shopping. First, consider how you will use the tool and whether

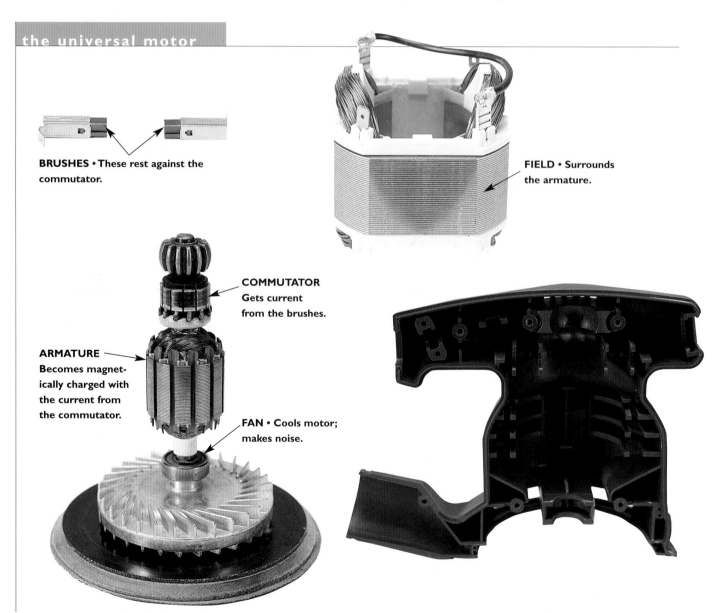

the universal motor

BRUSHES • These rest against the commutator.

FIELD • Surrounds the armature.

COMMUTATOR
Gets current
from the brushes.

ARMATURE
Becomes magnetically charged with the current from the commutator.

FAN • Cools motor;
makes noise.

it should be powered by an induction or universal motor. If you need your table saw to be portable or you're only turning it on for short times, a universal motor will do. But if your table saw is going to be on all the time, get an induction motor.

Things become more complicated when you start comparing one motor to another. Motors are measured differently by different manufacturers. Should you use horsepower? Amperage? Wattage? Motor efficiency? All of the above? The answer is that all these factors are related and all play a part in judging whether a motor has got a lot of guts or is just a loafer on the job.

First, let's clear the air about horsepower, which is the way you measure induction motors and some universal motors. It's almost a meaningless number, unfortunately. That's because there are several ways to measure horsepower, and this makes comparing two 1-hp motors almost impossible.

Some manufacturers measure horsepower with the motor under no load. Some measure horsepower as the saw almost reaches the point where it is about to stall — called the point of "breakdown torque." Some lock the motor in a dead stall, turn on the power and see how many amps the motor pulls from the outlet and calculate the horsepower from that. This is one way to measure "developed horsepower."

Developed horsepower is probably the least accurate measure of the motor's day-to-day abilities. When you lock the motor in a dead stall and turn it on, the motor will pull a lot more amps than normal because it's trying desperately to pull itself out of this stall.

Instead, try to find a "continuous-duty" horsepower rating, which is found on most high-quality induction motors. If the motor's nameplate doesn't state its horsepower rating is for continuous duty, ask the salesperson. If they don't know, have them find out, or call the manufacturer yourself.

Why is this so complicated? Keep in mind that there are a couple different formulas to calculate horsepower. One way is to multiply the rpm of the motor

DIFFERENT KINDS OF POWER FOR YOUR HOME SHOP

You probably know that most of your house is wired for 110-120 volts. And you might know that certain appliances, such as your electric range, dryer and big air conditioners, are wired for 220-240 volts. And perhaps you've heard about three-phase power. What's the difference… and which should you be using in your shop?

110-120 volts:
This is the standard current off of which most of your hand power tools run. And except for special circuits that power 240-volt appliances, this is the voltage to all the outlets in your house. Remember that voltage entering a house can fluctuate, so some people get 110 volts, some people get 120. Tools and appliances can handle a 12-volt variation, so don't worry.

220-240 volts:
To get this heavy-duty circuit, the electrician takes two lines from the main panel and one neutral line. These heavy-duty circuits are good for a variety of reasons. First, they need only half the amperage of 120-volt circuits, so you are less likely to trip a breaker or blow a fuse on a well-wired 240 circuit. Plus, 240 circuits are much less prone to voltage drops than 120 circuits. This means you can have a table saw that's more than 20 feet from your service box. Operating a motor at low voltage causes the torque to drop and the motor to heat up (shortening the life of the motor). Many induction motors can easily be switched over for 240

power. In the box on the motor where the electric cord goes in, there will be a diagram to show you how to reconnect the different leads. If you can afford the wiring change, do it. However, one myth about 240 power is that it is cheaper. Don't believe the myth. You buy power by the watt.

Three-phase power:
Look out your window at the power lines outside your house. The three power lines strung on the poles are carrying three-phase power. What's three-phase power? Well, the power coming into your house is single-phase power. This means that there's one electric pulse changing direction 60 times a second. Three-phase power has three of those pulses changing direction at slightly different times. The fluctuations are timed so that when one phase is at its lowest power, another phase is at its highest. The result is a very steady stream of energy. Three-phase power is typically used in factories, not homes. You need a special motor to run three-phase power, but three-phase motors are less expensive, extremely reliable and more efficient than single-phase motors. Three-phase power is not available to most residences. But you can purchase a "phase converter." Some manufacturers don't recommend static phase converters but say that rotary phase converters are OK. Bottom line — for the home shop — it's cheaper to buy a single-phase motor for a saw than it is to convert your juice to three-phase power.

by the amount of torque (which is in foot-pounds). Divide that number by 5,250 and you have a horsepower rating. Keep in mind that a universal motor's really high rpm skews this equation. The other horsepower formula involves the electricity going into the motor.

For this calculation, you need to know how amperage, voltage and wattage are related (this is that math we promised you). Almost every basic electricity textbook explains these different terms by comparing the electric

lines in your house to a water hose. Voltage is like water pressure. The more voltage you have, the more force with which the electricity moves through your wires. Amperage is like the amount of water in a hose. You can have the faucet on low or high. Wattage is harder to explain. It is, in electric terms, the amount of energy that a device consumes. You can calculate wattage by multiplying the amperage of a tool (usually found on the information plate on the motor) by the voltage

An employee at the Kosta Plant in Taiwan balances the armature on a universal motor. The plant assembles tools and tests motors for Delta Manufacturing.

Tip *The universal motors in most of your hand power tools will live longer if you follow this simple tip: blow clean air through the motor regularly. Universal motors suck a lot of air through them because the motors turn at a high speed and they have large fans to keep the motor from overheating. Think about your shop. Pretty dusty, isn't it? That dust is being sucked through your router and is slamming into your armature like a meteor shower. This dust can also build up, cause the motor to run hotter and shorten the life span of the tool. If you regularly blow compressed air through the vents of the tool, you'll dislodge the dust and keep your motor healthy. In addition to sawdust, the carbon-graphite material from the motor's brushes also builds up on the commutator. Blowing air through the tool helps dislodge that stuff, too, and this also prolongs the life of your tool.*

(which, for home-shop people in the U.S., is 120 volts or 240 volts). Why would you want to calculate wattage? Because 746 watts equals 1 hp.

So, with that formula you can attempt to calculate the actual horsepower (as opposed to the advertised horsepower). This is one of the most important aspects of this whole article. Remember it. Here's an example of how you can estimate how much horsepower a tool has compared to how much horsepower a tool says it has on the box: Does a 9-amp router live up to the 2-hp rating on its box? Let's see: 9 amps multiplied by 120 volts equals 1,080 watts of power. To get horsepower, we divide 1,080 watts by 746. The answer is 1.44 hp. Hmmm. You can probably guess that either this router will develop 2 hp just as it's ready to crash and burn, or that the manufacturer used that other horsepower equation, which uses rpm and torque, to calculate horsepower. And as pointed out earlier, universal motors in routers have very high rpm, which can skew that equation. (Our apologies to the gear heads here because we left out

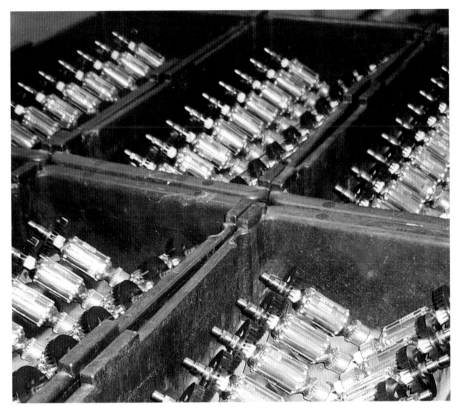

Assembled armatures and commutators at Makita's plant in Georgia.

some of the other complicated factors in calculating power, such as the power factor and line losses).

So if horsepower is a bogus measure, what does that leave us with? Amps. Amps tell you how much power a tool consumes, and that's the simplest way to compare similar motors, especially universal motors. Unfortunately, a lot of manufacturers tell us that the amperage on the nameplate is not always the amperage you get.

Three different 7-amp motors can all draw a different amount of current.

Even worse, amperage doesn't tell you how much of that energy is wasted. Here we're talking about the elusive "motor efficiency." Motor efficiency is not something advertised on many universal motors, but you can sometimes find it on the nameplate of induction motors. It is a percentage, usually between 50 percent and 80 percent, that explains how much of the amperage

going into the motor is converted into work coming out. When you shop for an induction motor, look for a motor with the highest efficiency, highest amps and best horsepower for the job.

If you can't tell a motor's efficiency, there are other ways to judge it in the store. One expert told us to peer through the vent fans in a tool with a universal motor to see if you can see the bars on the commutator. The smaller the bars, the better the motor. Smaller bars mean there are more coils in the armature winding, and that makes a smoother-running motor. If you can't see the commutator bars, there's still one final way to choose a motor: buy a trusted brand name.

Last year, our editor toured several manufacturing plants in Taiwan. At one facility, his tour guide pointed to a pile of rusting commutators sitting outside. Those, the guide explained, would be cleaned up, repaired and put into motors for off-brand tools. Installing used parts isn't something that happens just in Taiwanese off-brands. And don't assume this is a typical practice of Taiwanese manufacturers, because it isn't. Manufacturers of cheap motors anywhere can lower the cost of a tool by reducing the amount of iron and copper in a motor. This will lower the life span of the motor because all that metal acts as a heat sink to dissipate heat generated by the motor. They also can skimp on the brushes.

So do the math when you shop for motors. But even that can be misleading. One 14-amp chop saw can be $100 more than a similar-looking 14-amp chop saw. What's the difference? Probably the motor. Should that deter you from buying the cheap saw? No. If the tool won't get heavy use, a less expensive tool will allow you to spend that money somewhere else. But it should make you think twice about what you're buying and what you can expect in the long run.

INDUCTION VS. UNIVERSAL? YOU MAKE THE CALL

In the old days, table saws, planers and jointers had induction motors. Small tools had universal motors. Alas, that line has blurred in the last decade. Some manufacturers, such as Ryobi, DeWalt and others, put universal motors in their table saws. The universal motors are much smaller and are much less likely to stall in a cut, but they are much noisier and their life expectancy is shorter. Universal motors have also become the mainstay in portable planers — a tool that would have been a lot harder to design with

a huge induction motor driving it.

If you think you can run a table saw or planer for an extended period of time and it's powered by a universal motor, you'll be replacing the motor a lot sooner than you think. How can you determine if your tool has an induction or universal motor? Turn on the tool. A really noisy motor indicates it's probably a universal motor. If you're still not sure, look at the motor. Many universal motors have coin-opened hatches so you can easily change the brushes.

The New Rules of
Tool Buying

When your grandfather or maybe your dad started buying power tools, his choices were a lot simpler and a lot more limited. Only within the last 50 years have the tools to make home woodworking possible been readily available. Mass production, easily sourced quality imports and consumers with readily available disposable income have made it a shopper's paradise. Not only are the tools more readily available and affordable, they keep getting better. As with most technology, competition in the manufacturing of tools has kept prices down and instigated geometric improvements that have built quickly upon one another.

When Grandpa was shopping for a drill, he could get a Sears corded drill or one of the other two very similar models. Today, you have to decide whether you need a corded or cordless drill/driver, what voltage cordless drill, how many clutch positions are necessary, how many batteries, keyless chuck or not and whether or not it

About Us

WILLIAM ALDEN COMPANY®
Home of William Alden's Catalog For On-Line Shoppers

Catalog Request

Record

Folding Roller Stand

$19.99

PORTER·CABLE

Brad Nailer/Compressor Kit

$229.99

Secure On-Line Buying
Price Match Guarantee*
Quality You Expect From William Alden

5 Easy Steps To Navigate This Site:

1. Click on a manufacturer's logo
2. View feature item(s) of the day
3. Click "Order" to add to shopping cart, or...
4. Scroll down to view more products
5. Click "View Cart" to view ordered items

Now there are Two different Navigation styles for you to choose from by going to the Top Banner.

"For Best Viewing, Use Netscape Navigator V 4.6 or Internet Explorer Browser V 4.7 or Higher."

Click on the **Home** button in the top banner, left side, to come back here.

- Frequently Asked Questions (FAQ)
- About Shipping
- Can't Order Through The Shopping Cart ?

- About Pricing* & Description Errors
- About Privacy
- Contact Us

SHOPSITE4

OPEN MARKET
We ARE Internet Commerce™

WARRANTIES

Almost every woodworking power tool sold today is warranted against manufacturer's defects — some for six months, some for the lifetime of the tool. A warranty is certainly a good thing to have, but in general it isn't the most important factor in shopping for a tool. Most manufacturers consider "manufacturer's defects" to be just that — either it doesn't work straight out of the box or pieces are missing or broken. These defects are obvious very soon in the lifetime of a tool, but manufacturers offer six-month or one-year warranties in case the tool user doesn't get around to using the tool for a couple of months after buying it. Manufacturers also tend to give their customers the benefit of the doubt. If you bring a cordless drill back to the store after using it for two

months because the battery won't take a charge, they'll likely fix or replace it without question. On occasion, they'll even fix or replace a tool that's obviously been abused in the interest of good business. But that's not what the warranty is for. Even a lifetime warranty (as offered on Craftsman tools from Sears and Ridgid Tools from Home Depot) are for defects, not abuses. So while you should beware of tools with no warranty, any warranty should give you peace of mind that the tool you buy will perform as promised by the manufacturer or be replaced. If a lifetime warranty gives you better peace of mind, then follow your instincts, but make sure you're not buying a tool that isn't what you need just because it has a lifetime warranty.

---

should have a built-in bubble level or attached screw tips. Once you've answered those questions, you need to decide which of the 20 different companies selling drills are offering the best product for the price you want to pay. And, just to complicate things, you have to decide whether you want to shop at the local corner hardware store, the giant home center store, through mail-order catalogs or on the Internet. Grandpa, help!

Know What You Need

With so many tools and so many options available, having good information is even more critical. So, what's first? Recognize your need. Let's carry the drill analogy a little further. If you're building a deck, your need is to drive a lot of 3" deck screws. So turn to the section with information on cordless and corded drills chapters and determine which tools will best meet your needs.

Shop for Price

Next, head to the store, catalog or Internet to check the prices on the drills with the features you need. Once you have a selection to choose from, figure out how much further your money will go. If you can get more features from one manu-

facturer for about the same price as another manufacturer, good job ... you're ready to buy. But maybe not so fast. Let's discuss where you can shop and what each location has to offer.

Many Ways to Shop

Most woodworkers have a love/hate relationship with large home-center stores. They love the convenience, selection and price — but they find it very impersonal and hard to get accurate information about specific tools. Many smaller tool stores have been able to improve on the personal attention and information they offer in order to create a more comfortable shopping experience. Unfortunately, this personal touch comes with a little higher price. Catalogs and the Internet offer a simple way to find the best price on the tool you've already decided to buy — but if you needed advice, you were out of luck. Some new sites and catalogs are trying to offer buying information as well, but it's still remarkably impersonal and generic. What we all want is personal attention and specific information at large-volume, discount prices ... and it ain't there yet. So use this book and other tool information guides to help you decide what you need and want. If it's still not

enough, and some time spent with a knowledgeable tool salesman is still your first choice, don't abuse his livelihood by wasting his time and then heading for the Internet for the cheapest price. If you use his information, pay him his due (or 3-percent profit margin) and buy your tool from him.

Shipping not Included

While you're gloating over the $4 you saved by shopping around, make sure you remembered to add the shipping charges. While shipping charges for a cordless drill can be as little as $4, shipping a 15" planer can cost you up to $100. Sometimes it actually gets cheaper to buy more. Get over a certain price and the company will throw in the shipping costs. In either case, take the shipping into consideration before you make a final decision.

Help is Everywhere

If you don't have access to a local special interest tool store, but still want specific tool advice, keep your eyes open for tool reviews in woodworking magazines. Many will provide specific recommendations for tools they consider to be the best tool or the best bargain. Look carefully though, because the tool evaluators may not have the same tool needs as you do.

Another way to get specific tool advice is to reach out over the Internet to other tool shoppers and owners. Via discussion groups and newsgroups, you can ask other woodworkers about specific brands and models. In the best case scenario, you'll hear from someone who has owned the exact tool you're considering and who can tell you the good and bad points. You should be able to get at least an opinion of the brand of tools and whether they will be up to your task. Again, be selective in taking what you read or hear to heart — the chances of finding a person using the tools you are interested in, for the same task you're performing, are pretty slim.

Should You Buy Professional Tools?

Know the difference between a tool built for occasional use and a tool built for a daily workout

By Randy Caillier

Randy Caillier is a regional service manager for a major tool company and has been involved in the power tool and equipment industry since 1978.

Most woodworkers know you should have the right tool for the job. But choosing the right power hand tool can sometimes be confusing — particularly when the different tools you are considering are made by the same manufacturer, but have wildly different price tags. For example, you can buy a $39 jigsaw or a $160 jigsaw from the same manufacturer. Both will cut wood, but will the $160 jigsaw cut wood four times better than the $39 tool? Probably not.

So, in order to decide which power tool is right for you, it's good to understand the difference between inexpensive tools and expensive ones. In a broad sense, manufacturers make tools for two types of users. On one hand are the occasional users. These are homeowners, do-it-yourselfers and part-time hobbyists who use power tools occasionally. On the other end of the scale are professional users. These are carpenters or commercial woodworkers who use their tools every day and demand the most from them.

If the situation were that black and white, things would be simple. However, many occasional users are demanding shoppers and have the money to purchase better tools than they might need. This two-tier scenario also doesn't take into consideration the advanced home woodworker who wants "pro" tools or the professional who only needs a chop saw once a month.

In some cases, manufacturers do not clearly identify their two separate design groups. Some use the same tool color across their line, and they use the same marketing terminology in ads and catalogs. Other companies produce tools under two different brand names: one for the home user and one for the professional. For example, Black & Decker and DeWalt are part of the same company, but DeWalt tools are built and marketed specifically for the professional market. Bosch builds tools for the professional user, but its sister company markets a line of home tools under the Skil nameplate.

Recognizing the difference between "pro" and home tools isn't easy when

you're in the store. One good indicator used to be the features on the tool, but even the less expensive tools now offer more features. So the place to start is with the price tag. A $39 drill is built differently from a $139 drill. The line blurs again, however, when you start comparing high-end tools to other high-end tools, such as a $140 jigsaw and a $250 jigsaw. Sometimes you don't get what you pay for at that level.

Fit and Finish

One in-store technique for separating "pro" tools from home tools is looking at the fit and finish of a tool. Are the seams tight or rough? Do the switches, knobs or levers operate smoothly and with precision? Does the outer surface of the tool have sharp edges? Is the finish or paint bubbled, chipped or uneven? Does the battery slide in and out of the tool easily? Does the router base adjust smoothly? These are things that can help you identify whether a tool has been engineered for home or professional use.

The fact is, most of the differences

between tools are internal and, unless you're an engineer and have the opportunity to tear apart a tool, you won't know the difference. Here's a look at some of the internal differences between "pro" tools and home tools.

Bearings and Bushings

Manufacturers anticipate occasional users will put less wear and tear on the parts, so they use parts rated for a shorter lifespan to keep the price affordable. (Price is a strong selling point for occasional users.) Instead of ball or needle bearings, they'll use bushings or plain bearings to center a rotating shaft in a tool. Bushings provide some wear protection and centering for the tool's rotating shaft. They are usually made from a single piece of metal or nylon, and they have no moving parts.

Ball or needle bearings, on the other hand, are made from several pieces of steel, providing high levels of centering accuracy and finer tolerances. Also, ball-and-needle-type bearings protect the rotating shaft from wear better than a bushing. Ball bearings can handle rotating shafts that thrust as well as spin (called a radial load). Roller or

Professional tools use gears that are machined several times to a fine tolerance. Home tools might use straight-cut or powdered gears that are inexpensive to make. Though these inexpensive gears are less desirable, their quality has been increasing in recent years with strides in manufacturing technology.

needle bearings are built for handling only radial loads — but they can handle huge loads. Both types of bearings usually cost much more than bushings or plain bearings.

Ball and needle bearings are considered almost standard in a professional tool. An instance where this would not hold true would be for the rollers on a belt sander, because the dusty environment would reduce the effectiveness of ball bearings.

You're not going to be able to determine what type of bearing or bushing is used in a tool while you're shopping in the store, but the price is usually a good indicator of what's inside.

Gears

The amount of machining performed on a gear affects the performance and quality of a tool. The tighter the gears, the less play in the mechanism and, therefore, less wasted energy as the tool operates. Tighter tolerance also reduces wear on the gears, extending the life of the tool.

To create a quality gear, manufacturers generally have to go through multiple machining steps. Each step adds to the cost of the gear, but it does improve the quality of the gear match.

At one time, tools for the occasional user could be identified by straight-cut or powdered gears. Straight-cut refers to a rough-cast gear that is machined in a single step to keep the overall cost of the gear low. A powdered gear is made by pressing powdered steel into a mold under high pressure — which produced a gear that was less expensive and had a shorter life-span. Today's technology now produces powdered gears that rival machined steel gears for precision. Many manufacturers are now using these improved powdered gears — but not all. In some cases, low-tolerance, single-run and poorer-grade powdered gears can actually be heard as a raspy metal-rubbing-on-metal sound when the tool winds down.

Tool Housings

When plastic housings on hand tools started to become the norm, they were

Ball bearings or needle bearings are one indicator of a "pro" tool. How will you know if your tool has these bearings? You won't unless you take the thing apart.

often considered to be less durable. However, with today's technology, plastic housings are all over the map. Some are still somewhat flimsy. But many quality professional tools now have glass-filled nylon housings that are extremely durable and also insulate against excess heat produced by the motor.

Two-piece, clam-shell motor or tool housings are found in both professional and occasional-use tools. As the term implies, the whole tool housing is split in half, with a left and a right side. For the manufacturer, the clam-shell tool is easier to assemble at the plant, and any step saved in the manufacturing process reduces the final cost of the tool. As the halves go down the line, the tool components can easily be placed into the open half, and at the end of the assembly process the two halves are screwed together.

If there is a weakness of this housing style, it occurs when the tool's bearing seats also are created in two pieces. For a bearing or bushing to be most effective, it needs to remain stationary in its housing location (or bearing seat). When you apply heavy loads to a split or two-piece bearing seat, they may flex apart — causing the exterior of the bushing or bearing to slip or spin with the rotating shaft. As this happens, the bearing or bushing is less effective. The worst scenario occurs when the slipping or spinning of the bushing or bearing race (the bearing exterior) is excessive. The plastic bearing seats begin to melt, causing the shaft tolerance to alter, which leads to major tool failure.

Switch Covers

Dust, liquids and other debris can enter the switch and cause its contacts to short out, which is one of the first things that usually goes wrong with a tool.

To protect against this, some manufacturers place a dust cover or "boot" on the switch. A quality rubber switch dust cover is often designed into the professional-user tool models (and more and more into home tools). You can't always see this difference in the store. More and more, professional tools offer an internally sealed switch to keep dust out without impeding access to the switch.

Uncovered or unsealed switches are fine for lower-usage tools because of the cleaner work environment and lower frequency of use.

Cords

Occasional-use tools often have a plastic, one-piece, molded cord guard, while professional tools have a two-piece rubber cord with a separate guard. The one-piece plastic cord is acceptable for home use because of the tool's infrequent use (causing less stress on the power cord) and less extreme temperature demands. A rubber cord on a professional tool allows more flexibility during normal or cold weather use, while the plastic cord can become stiff and unmanageable, even crack or break, in cold weather use.

A one-piece cord is less expensive because it allows manufacturers to quickly install the cord during assembly, reducing the overall cost of the tool.

Warranties

One thing you can check in the store is the warranty offered on a tool. But does a longer warranty mean a better tool? Not always. Professionals notice problems with their tools quickly after purchase, so a 90-day or six-month warranty on a professional tool is pretty standard. A two-year warranty gives the occasional user the opportunity to use a tool a few times (or for the first time after a year or so) to discover defects. This gives the occasional user a fair shake at being covered by the warranty.

In most cases, more important than the warranty is the manufacturer's reputation for standing behind its tools. Quality manufacturers take a look at warranty requests on an individual basis and usually support their tool unless an obvious abuse has occurred.

Brushes

Another visible indicator of a high-quality universal motor tool is the presence of an external hatch that allows you to easily replace the brushes. (Except for cordless tools, in which external brush access is rare). Professional tools see enough use to require new brushes, so manufacturers make this maintenance procedure easy to do in the field. Tools for the home user don't usually have these hatches because it's unlikely the tool will be used enough during its lifetime to warrant new brushes.

Motors

A tool's motor is difficult to evaluate in the store. Motors come from many sources and the country of origin isn't always the sign of a good or bad motor. Some motors for power hand tools are rated in horsepower or developed horsepower. Ignore this rating. Check out the amperage rating on the motor's information plate. This indicates how much current the motor pulls from the wall and is a better indication of the tool's power. However, amperage can also be difficult to understand. So, the truth is, there's no perfect way to compare motors. (See chapter titled "What You Must Know About Motors" for more information.)

So Should You Buy a "Pro" Tool?

It's not fair to say that tools for the occasional user are not worth buying. As a matter of fact, if you honestly place your power tool work requirements into the occasional-use category, some can be a good value.

On the other hand, if you plan to

DIFFERENCES BETWEEN "PRO" AND HOME TOOLS

Bushings and Bearings
"Pro" tools use ball or needle bearings. Some home tools use bushings or plain bearings.

Gears
"Pro" tools use highly machined gears. Some home tools use straight-cut or powdered gears.

Housing
Some "pro" tools use a molded one-piece case to support bearings. Some home tools (and "pro" tools) use a two-piece clam-shell design.

Switch
"Pro" tools use a cover on the tool's switch to keep dust out. Some home tools don't have a dust cover.

Cords
"Pro" tools use a rubber cord that has a separate guard. Home tools tend to have a cord and cord guard molded into one piece.

Warranty
Home tools tend to have a longer warranty than "pro" tools.

Brush Hatches
"Pro" tools have coin-opened hatches that let you get to the brushes in a universal motor tool. Some home tools do not.

---

make a living with your power tools, or if you know you will be using them on a more-than-occasional basis at home under heavy work conditions, consider buying the professional-user tools. This will keep you out of the repair shops and on the job.

A ir tools in a woodworking shop can be time savers, provide a level of quality usually beyond a home woodworker, and even save you money. But more than most tools in your shop, you should look at air tools as more a tool system rather than as individual tools. Determine what your needs are (and will be) and buy accordingly so you won't have to upgrade along the way.

There's a pretty broad range of quality in air tools and compressors. Some brand names have been around for a long time, others are fairly new and likely imported. As with all tools, your frequency of use should direct the level of tool you require. In general, the best price is not the best tool, but may do well for your particular needs.

Porter-Cable's model #CFBN125A kit includes a compressor, brad nailer, 25 feet of hose and all of the necessary couplings to get you started.

What's Out There

Generally, air tools fall into three categories: compressors, fastening tools and finishing tools. Compressors provide the air power to run all of your air tools, and must be purchased by capacity according to what type of tools and needs you have in your shop.

Fastening tools, such as air nailers and staplers, provide a speed and reliability in construction that is the standard in most commercial woodworking. However, they aren't a replacement for traditional woodworking joinery, as they can leave telltale holes. But, for at least half of many woodworking projects, where strength and unmarred surfaces aren't critical, air fasteners can make a two-day job into a one-day job. Air-powered brads and staples also provide temporary and immediate holding power, dramatically reducing the need for expensive clamps and downtime while glue dries.

Air-powered finishing tools offer superior finishing capabilities to the home woodworker, enabling you to use the commercial norm of a sprayed lacquer finish, which offers high durability, speed of application and even consistency.

So Why Aren't We All Using Air-Powered Tools Already?

Mostly price. There are different levels of air tools, defined predominantly by the amount of air required to run them. For example, air fasteners can be powered by relatively small, affordable compressors, but air sanders require a fairly large amount of air to operate the tool continuously. This means a larger, more expensive compressor.

Compressors

Compressors are the heart or, more appropriately, the lungs of any air tool system. They not only provide air — most are designed to regulate the airflow to provide the most efficient performance of the tool. If you've taken a look at compressors, you may have come to the conclusion they all look an awfully lot alike. You're not mistaken. Many are produced in the same factories overseas and labeled privately for different retail markets.

Don't assume that an imported tool is not as good — a compressor is a fairly simple tool, and can be easily produced at a reasonable price.

Capacity

There are three basic size models likely to be found in a home woodworking shop. Larger capacity 60- or 80-gallon tank models offer a reliable, continuous flow of air for all air tools, including finishing tools and air sanders. Also, because they can store larger amounts of air, the motor doesn't need to run as often, reducing wear on the pump and motor.

The medium-size 20- to 30-gallon semi-portable models will provide reasonable airflow for many applications including finishing with proper care. Air sanders and air fasteners will be no problem with these models, but, depending on your application, they may run more often.

The smaller portable models (usually 4- to 6-gallon capacity) offer proper airflow for most air fastening tools, and could be used for limited sanding applications. They would not be recommended for finishing, as the airflow would not keep up with the demands of the tool.

CFM v. PSI:

This is a critical feature in determining which compressor you should buy. Compressor performance is rated by the cubic feet of air produced per minute (cfm). Most air tools will specify the required amount of cfm to allow the tool to operate at peak performance. Closely tied to the cfm rating is

Makita's model MAC500 1½-hp "hot dog" compressor.

the pounds per square inch of pressure (psi) produced by the compressor. These two statistics work hand-in-hand, as the cfm will drop or rise depending on the psi required. This is especially critical when using a compressor for finishing.

In general, air nailers require 2 to 6 cfm at around 90 psi, sanders (as well as drills) use between 10 to 25 cfm at 90 psi, and finishing spray guns need between 5 to 8 cfm at 90 psi.

Amperage Draw

Compressors are amperage pigs. Even the smallest compressors will demand 10 to 15 amps to operate. When you move up into slightly larger models, a standard 15 amp home circuit may not be sufficient to allow the compressor to operate. For the largest compressor, you will likely need 220-volt power to run the machine, pulling 20, and even up to 40, amps to operate. After determining what cfm you need for the tools you want to use, find out which compressors will provide that cfm level, then check the compressor's amperage requirements. Now compare that number to your situation at home. Remember, even if you have a 20-amp circuit,

Campbell-Hausfeld's 6½-hp VT7610 compressor.

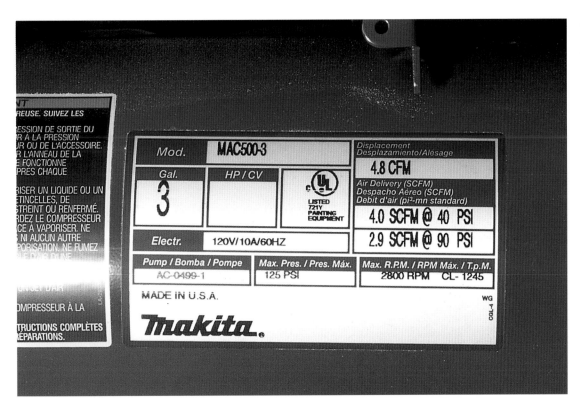

A label on each compressor shows you the cfm vs. psi rating.

Emglo's 30-gallon compressor, model GC3E-30V.

adequate to operate the compressor, you may not be able to operate other electrical appliances on that circuit at the same time.

Oil or Oilless

Just as it sounds, some compressors are designed with a lubricating finish on the moving parts to allow the compressor to operate without needing lubricating oil added every so often. Which is better? Compressors that require oil operate more quietly than oilless units. They do require more careful routine maintenance and, if not properly filtered from finishing equipment, oil may show up in finishing materials. On the other hand, oilless compressors will require a pump rebuild or replacement after a few thousand hours of operation. In our experience, oil-lubricated compressors perform very adequately when properly maintained.

Portability

From personal experience, we recommend that you not consider all smaller compressors portable. In the small capacity category, the "pancake" and single-tank models are usually light

enough to be picked up and moved as necessary, but the twin-tank models become a bit more back-breaking. When you move into the mid-capacity category, most manufacturers have added wheels. This does make them portable — unless you have to negotiate steps. The large capacity compressors should be bolted in place and left alone. Depending on how you plan to use your compressor, try moving your compressor before purchasing to see if your back is up to the task.

In Compressors, Look For:

- Capacity. Figure out what task you'll be using the tool for, then choose the necessary capacity.
- Requirements for cfm. Check the air tools you'll be using for their cfm requirements, then match them to the compressor.
- Amperage. Make sure your house or shop has enough amperage to support the compressor you want.
- Oil or Oilless. Choose whichever is more in-line with your needs.
- Size. Consider whether you will be moving the compressor, or bolting it to the floor.

Air Nailers and Staplers

Air fasteners run the gamut from 23-gauge, ½"-long micro pinners to 16d 3½" framing nailers. Along the way are a wide variety of air staplers ranging in use from upholstery work to commercial cabinetry assembly. For the average woodworker, a couple of tools will work well for almost every application. Brad nailers will fire 16-gauge brads ranging in length from ½" to 2", providing adequate fastening power for 90 percent of all woodworking tasks. Air staplers are available in similar length ranges and provide extra holding power for larger furniture pieces which will see more rigorous use.

Most home woodworkers can get by with one or two air tools for most of their woodworking tasks. A brad nailer with a fastener range of ½" to 2" will cover most tasks, with either a headless pinner or finish stapler for more specialty needs. You may ask why you shouldn't use staples in all applications, since they provide better holding power. Staples double the potential for splitting a piece of wood, and will leave a much larger crown visible on the surface of your project. In general, staples are preferred in plywood or particleboard construction that will be hidden from view, covered by laminate or puttied and painted.

As with compressors, there are several brands available. All but the most high-end tools are an import. Recognized brand-name tools are the most reliable, but many of the off-brand tools are likely to be a good value for the occasional user.

Porter-Cable's BN125A brad nailer fires 18-gauge brads from ⅝" to 1¼" long.

Hitachi's N3804AB finish stapler fires ¼"-crown staples ranging from ½" to 1½" long.

Depth-of-Drive Adjustment

Depending on the amount of psi dialed in on your compressor, the fastener will drive to a different depth in different materials. Optimally, the fastener should sink slightly below the surface of the wood, leaving enough of a depression to hold putty if required. While this depth can be adjusted on most compressors, that's not always convenient in the middle of an assembly. Because of this, some air nailers and staplers will offer a depth-of-drive adjustment on the tool itself. This allows you to adjust the depth at the work, not the compressor. While not a requirement on a tool, it's an attractive feature to look for when comparing costs.

Visible Load Indicator

Many manufacturers are now including visible load indicators on their tools. These offer a window on the clip to indicate when only a couple of fasteners are left in the gun. There's nothing worse than getting halfway through a tricky assembly to find you've been shooting "blanks," and your last glued-up piece falls off. While most of us are

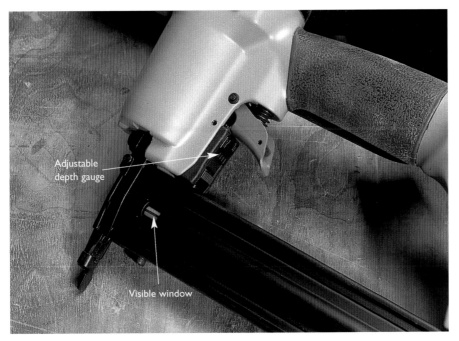

Adjustable
depth gauge

Visible window

Close-up of the depth gauge and visible window for checking the number of staples left.

capable of opening the slide on a tool to check the number of fasteners left, a visible indicator makes it a little easier. Again, not a requirement in choosing a tool, but handy.

Weight and Material

It used to be the axiom that a plastic tool was a bad tool. While that still may be true, the definition of "plastic" has adjusted to technological advances. Today's glass-filled plastics and polymers provide durability and comfort in a tool light enough to be used for long periods of time without any muscle fatigue. Aluminum offers these same attributes with the increased benefit of one-piece milling for improved tool performance. So, when purchasing, don't ignore lightweight tools. Modern construction materials have provided us with quality tools at an easy-to-handle heft.

Oilless or Directional Exhaust?

The vast majority of air-fastening tools designed for the home woodworker require that a small amount of lubricating oil be added to the tool before each use. This keeps the cylinder operating smoothly, but can cause problems if the exhaust from the tool allows some of the lubricating oil to stain the wood.

While this is a more rare occurrence than most marketing information would have us believe, there are two ways to avoid the problem altogether. If available, a tool requiring no oil quickly solves the problem. These are rare in today's market and tend to be more expensive. Another option is a directional exhaust which allows the tool user to turn the exhaust blast away from any sensitive wood surfaces. These are both nice features to consider, but we wouldn't use either as a criteria to not buy a tool if missing.

Trigger Configuration

Less common in today's models is a non-sequential firing mechanism. This trigger mechanism allows the user to hold the trigger in and, by tapping the nose safety of the gun on the material, fire repeatedly without releasing the trigger. This non-sequential, or bump-fire, option is a valuable asset when using a roofing nailer or framing nailer, but is a deficit in the home woodworking arena. Beyond the potential for accidents (bumping into legs, etc.), bump-firing tools are notorious for double-firing in rapid succession into the same area or a piece. This can mar, split or cause "blow-outs" in the side of the material. Some import models will

still include this type of trigger, but we recommend sequential firing tools.

Another trigger option is the type of safety provided. Some tools will use a "nose" safety which must be depressed against the wood before firing. Another option is a double trigger, in which first one, then a second, trigger must be pulled to fire the gun. This is a personal preference — there are benefits to both. The nose safety tends to be the safer of the two options, but it can keep the gun from getting into tight positions. The double-trigger safety allows the gun to get right up against a corner to fire. One new option on the market is from Porter-Cable, with a nose safety located at the rear of the nose, providing the best of both worlds.

Kits

A happy option now available from a number of manufacturers is the brad nailer kit. Offering a brad nailer (unfortunately of a limited fastener range such as ⅝" to 1"), a portable compressor and necessary hoses, these kits allow you to enter the world of air tools with a purchase of around $250 to $300. If air fastening is your primary reason to check out this category, these kits are a great deal. If you're considering air sanders or finishing, you'll be better off buying a larger compressor and piecing out the other tools.

In Air Nailers and Staplers, Look For:

- Nails, staples or both. Determine your needs.
- Depth of drive. Is the tool adjustable? If so, this is a nice feature to have.
- Visible load indicator. This will make sure you don't run out of nails in the middle of a job.
- Weight. Will you be using the tool over your head all day? Buy a light one!
- Oil or oilless. Oilless is best, but expect to pay more.
- Sequential triggers. These are safest, and are adequate for most woodworking.

Air Finishing Equipment

The tool involved in air finishing is primarily the spray gun. The other pieces are regulators, hoses and air filtration and ventilation products which should be determined with the assistance of a finishing equipment dealer. The spray gun itself is a little easier to comprehend.

A spray gun is essentially a tool to mix compressed air with the liquid finishing product (lacquer, shellac, etc.) in a proper balance to spray the material evenly over your project. They are available in a couple of simple designs: a cup gun using a 1-quart cup mounted directly to the spray nozzle, or a spray pot with a 1- to 5-gallon material pot attached to the spray nozzle by hoses. The cup gun is the cheaper option, and eliminates the hoses, so there is less chance of the hoses becoming gummed-up with old lacquer. You can also change the type of material used (paint,

lacquer or shellac) without cleaning the changing hoses.

On the other hand, the cup gun will need to be refilled often on larger finishing projects. If you haven't premixed a large batch of finish, the sheen, color or consistency can differ between fills. Also, cup guns can become material-starved if turned or tipped at extreme angles. Since the spray pot keeps the material sitting on the ground, the nozzle is able to be moved into more extreme positions, making finishing hard-to-reach spaces a lot easier.

As with every tool in this book, some manufacturer's products will be better than others. Stick to a known brand name, and build your entire finishing system from the same manufacturer's products. If they don't offer such accessories, you may be asking for trouble down the road. As always, if it's too good a deal to be true, don't buy it.

There are a number of things to consider before heading in the direction of spray-finishing gear, as well. Finishing equipment requires a great deal of air movement, demanding a larger com-

pressor — and a higher price. Beyond the need for more air, spraying a finish also requires a commitment to health and safety — meaning an appropriate ventilation system where you are spraying. This doesn't mean a box fan in a window. It means creating a proper finishing booth that can properly exchange the air and provide filters to trap offspray material and reduce pollutants.

HVLP

While an air tool of sorts, an HVLP (high-volume low-pressure) finishing system doesn't require a compressor and can be an answer to using some air tools without having to buy a very large compressor. By buying a compressor adequate to your fastening and sanding requirements, then adding an HVLP system, all your air needs can be met. For about the same price as a large compressor, an HVLP system will allow you to apply spray finishes to your work with just a little retraining. An HVLP system uses less forced air to move the finishing material onto the project. There is less overspray, so the material lasts longer and is less messy and environmentally hazardous. It isn't exactly the same finish as a complete spray-finishing system, but with a little patience

Wagner HVLP 1-qt. non-bleeder cup gun.

Wagner 2600 HVLP system, with three-stage turbine.

and practice, the results are more than acceptable for less money, with fewer equipment requirements. They should still be used with appropriate ventilation and a spray booth is still a good idea, but it's not absolutely necessary.

A variation on HVLP is a conversion gun, which basically uses a compressor to provide the same low-material and low-offspray capacities. This is a more expensive option, but serves an ecological purpose while offering a finishing system closer to commercial air systems.

Costs for HVLP systems range from around $300, up to $800. Unless your environmental requirements demand HVLP, the higher-priced systems may not be a better option over a standard compressed air system. Features to look for in HVLP systems are the number of stages used in the turbines to force the air through the gun. In general, the more stages, the better the performance. A three-stage turbine is a nice machine, though a single-turbine system will provide an adequate finish in many cases. Also, HVLP systems move more air which requires a larger-diameter hose. Check the flexibility and weight of the hose to make sure using it won't be like dragging around a suitcase while you're trying to spray.

HVLP is an alternative to more expensive and environmentally awkward finishing systems, but there is a lot to learn. Again, check with a finishing systems professional, or read more books about finishing to determine the right system for you.

In Air Finishing Equipment, Look For:

- Cup gun or pot. Determine your needs.
- Hoses. Get good hoses and match them to your finishing needs.
- HVLP. Is your compressor up to the task? Or do you need HVLP? If so, turbine is your best option.

The Coin Flip:

For the average woodworker, a portable 15-amp compressor will run a nail gun very adequately. That gun (or at least the first one) should be a brad nailer with a ⅝" to 2" range. Buy other brad nailers or staplers later. Don't worry about air sanders unless you're doing this for a living. For the best way into air finishing, choose a mid-level turbine two- or three-stage HVLP system. A high-pressure system is great, but it takes a lot more equipment and space — so, again, this is a "pro" or future option.

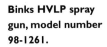

Binks HVLP spray gun, model number 98-1261.

HOSES

Any air-finishing system is only as efficient as the hoses that move the air. There are two basic types of hoses: air hoses and fluid hoses, and there is a difference. Air and fluid hoses are not designed to be interchangeable, so buy the right type of hose.

Air hoses are used to connect the finishing gun or pot to the main air connection, whether directly to the compressor or to a separate regulator attached to the air line, and then to the compressor. Air hoses can be used to connect the finish pot to the gun. If you're using a cup gun, this hose isn't necessary; they're already attached.

Fluid hoses connect the finishing pot to the spray gun, unless you're using a cup gun.

The best air hoses for finishing are flexible, rated to well beyond the psi required (usually 250 psi) of the finishing operation, and preferably only as long as is necessary to improve the efficiency of the compressor — but don't make it too short. They can be purchased in PVC or rubber. PVC is usually cheaper, but less flexible. Rubber hoses are resistant to solvents used in finishing fluids.

When spraying finishes, the fluid hose can be one of the areas where problems occur. If not properly cleaned after each use, finishing material can solidify or dry in the fluid line. When the gun is next used, small pieces of the old fluid material can be spit out onto the work surface.

Also, if using color-tinted finishes or paints, the residue or pigments from the finish can remain in the hose and taint later finishing fluids. Either clean the fluid hose very well in these situations, or use separate hoses for each such color-finishing application.

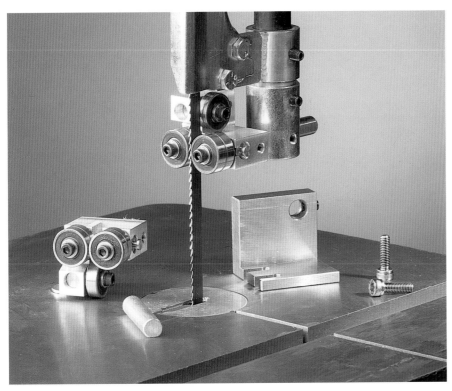

Carter brand high-precision, after-market band saw guides.

Why You Want One

After the table saw, the band saw is a workshop must-have. Band saws bring the versatility and utility you need to slice those graceful, sweeping curves found on many woodworking projects. Band saws are the shop tool for safe re-sawing, for sawing thick wood into sizes useful for projects, for cutting swooping outside curves and for following templates when making multiple identical parts. Even very complex shapes such as Queen Anne furniture legs are easy to make with band saws because of their curve-cutting ability in thick stock.

Band saws cut more than just wood. They're practical tools for cutting nonferrous metals and plastics of many kinds, provided you use the appropriate blades (some wood blades work well with plastics, but cutting metals requires special blades).

A band saw is basically just an endless steel band (the blade) rotating around two or three wheels. Because the blade is always traveling downward and away from you, there's no danger of kickback. As long as you watch where your fingers are, a band saw is a very safe workshop tool.

PUBLIC LIBRARY
DANVILLE, ILLINOIS

Understanding the Features

Band Saw Size

Although band saws come in different configurations and styles, you can't necessarily go by the stated size. For two-wheel band saws, size is usually quoted on the depth of the throat (the distance from the blade to the column or post behind it) or the size of the wheels. Typically, a 12" band saw will have wheels that measure almost (but not quite) 12". Whether throat depth or wheel size is used, manufacturers round up the number.

A three-wheel saw, however, is a different animal. The triangular blade path and the three smaller wheels allow for a very deep throat that gives you a greater cutting capacity. But, typically, a three-wheel band saw is designed for lighter duty than a two-wheel saw of equal throat depth. That means a 14" three-wheel model probably isn't going to be as powerful as its two-wheeled cousin.

Confusing things even further is the fact that some manufacturers quote their band saw size according to their depth of cut, which means the thickest material it can handle. This measurement comes from the distance from the saw table to the top of the blade guide. So, when comparing saws, be sure you know how the size measurements were calculated.

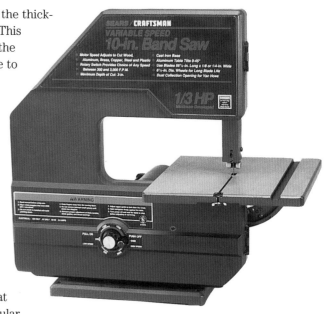

An older model of a Craftsman three-wheel band saw.

Two-wheel vs. Three-wheel

Two-wheel saws are more common than three-wheel saws, with the blade rotating in an oval pattern around two wheels in vertical orientation. A three-wheel saw adds a wheel that sends the blade on a triangular route. These sharper turns sometimes mean reduced blade life and it can be harder to get the blade to track properly. The upside is that a three-wheel saw, by the nature of its design, can have a very deep throat in a relatively compact saw. Most of the three-wheel saws you'll encounter will be benchtop models.

Riser Kits

Some two-wheel band saws let you add an optional riser kit to extend the depth of cut. Since predicting the future is a tough job, we'd recommend purchasing the riser kit even if you don't immediately use it. It's nice to have it available, and keep in mind that you'll need longer blades to be able to use it.

Blades

The key to success with a band saw is proper blade choice and, be warned, there are a lot of choices for you to ponder. There's no one size that's perfect for everything, so expect to buy three to six different types of blades to have on hand for various tasks.

The rules of thumb for blade choice are these:

• The tighter the curve, the narrower the blade.

• The harder the material being cut, the finer the pitch (more teeth per inch).

• Fewer teeth and a wider blade for fast cutting, ripping or resawing. Keep in mind, though, that the band saw can't match a table saw for ripping because of the tendency of even wide band saw blades to follow the grain of the wood.

• Blade widths vary from ⅛" up to ¾" with size stops all along the line. Optimal blade sizes vary by band saw size, so plan on experimenting to find the setups that work best for your projects and saw. For example, even though some 14" band saws claim you can use a ¾"-wide blade, this wide blade comes under a lot of stress making the tight turns around a 14" wheel, and thus breaks more often than a narrower blade.

What's Out There

Like most woodworking tools, band saws come in floor and benchtop sizes, in either two or three-wheel versions. Two-wheel models are by far the more common and popular. Three-wheel models use an extra wheel to set up a triangular blade path that deepens the saw's cutting capacity without adding a lot of extra size to the saw. As a result, most three-wheel models you'll see are benchtop designs.

Tip *Install better blade guides. The metal guides offered as standard equipment on most band saws do just fine if carefully adjusted and frequently checked. For greater service at low cost, graphite-impregnated guides are the best, and Cool Blocks is one popular brand. These guides ride directly against the saw blade, reducing deflection, giving you a straighter cut. Installation takes only minutes, although you'll be replacing them as they wear out. If you're really planning on getting your money's worth out of a new band saw, either buy one with ball bearing guides standard or purchase them as options. They need less frequent adjustment, last a long, long time, are easy to install and, unfortunately, are a bit costly. Carter Guides are the best known, but BandRollers, which fit in the present guide holders, cost about half as much. Cool Blocks will set you back about $15 a set, but must be changed when worn down too far. BandRollers cost about $70, while Carter Guides will make a $150 dent in your checking account. See our Sources page for more information.*

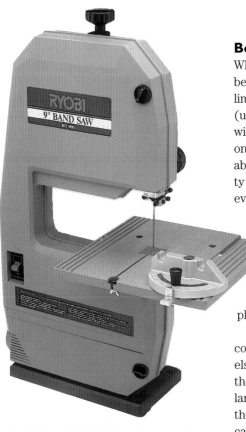

Ryobi 9" model BS900 benchtop band saw.

Benchtop Models

When both money and space are tight, benchtop models will do the job within limits. Curve cutting in thinner stock (up to 2") is often nearly as good as with floor models, but template cutting on multiple pieces is not. Resawing ability is also not as great nor is capacity as high. Usually you've got less of everything — power, throat depth, features and adjustability.

Two-wheel benchtop models can cost as little as $200 and still handle most light-duty tasks. For those with modest needs in a band saw, there are plenty of suitable models.

Benchtop three-wheel band saws compare favorably to two-wheel models. Resawing power and capacity is either equal or a bit higher, plus you get larger stock-cutting capacity because of the design. Blades on three-wheelers can be harder to adjust, with tracking being a special problem (one more wheel to align). Blade tension settings can also be more difficult to get right, and blade life may be shorter because of the tighter turns it has to make over those three wheels.

You'll find a wide range of benchtop saws and an equally broad range of prices and features. If you need a benchtop band saw because of space limitations or because you know your cutting needs will always be light-duty, spend the money to buy one of the more expensive and feature-filled brand names like Delta, Craftsman, Ridgid, Woodtek, Inca or Grizzly. The name brands will give you the best combination of features, cutting accuracy, warranty, options and longevity at a reasonable price.

BUILD A SIMPLE RESAW JIG

Of course, you can buy special resaw jigs for your band saw, or you can save a few dollars by making this shop-built version.

Rip a piece of hardwood to the width of the wood you expect to be re-sawing in height. For a 4" resaw, you need to rip a 4"- or 3-½"-wide piece of wood that's about 12" long.

Cut two 45-degree angles on one end of the wood, bringing the ¾" end to a moderately sharp point.

Cut a sweeping curve with the band saw in the back of the piece, leaving a 1"- to 2"-tall tail long enough to allow easy clamping to the band saw table.

Align the resaw jig so it leads the band saw blade by ⅛" to ¼" and is the distance away from the blade that you need to resaw in thickness. Note that this isn't finished thickness, so allow some extra for dressing the resulting board with plane or sandpaper.

In Benchtop Models, Look For:

- Frame rigidity. Does it seem to be a tool or a toy?
- Clean wheel castings (metal is preferable to urethane wheels).
- Is it stable when standing upright on a flat surface?
- Does the table adjust easily and lock down solidly?
- Does the height guide move easily and lock solidly?
- Is the blade easy to tension?
- How much does it weigh? Lighter may be better if you're going to be moving it around a lot in your shop.

Delta 14" band saw, model 28-280.

JET's JWBS-14CS 14" floor-model band saw.

Floor-Model Band Saws

Floor-model band saws are the small-shop champs, with sizes starting around 12" and going up to 24", although you'd only see ones that big in commercial shops. Floor model prices start at around $300, but expect to pay closer to $500 to get enough power and features to be happy.

Floor-model frames are of steel or cast iron. The more sturdy, massive and rigid the frame, the better. The 14" and 15" models are the most popular, offering an excellent cost/performance ratio. Saws this size can tackle many resawing jobs because a full-height cut on a 14" band saw is about 6". Models that offer optional riser kits for the neck of the saw, can raise the cut and resaw capacity to 12". Floor-model band saws in the 14" to 15" range have ¾ to 1½ horsepower motors, enough power to easily cut delicate patterns and tight or sweeping curves. If you're doing a lot of resawing though, you'll want the most power you can get.

Floor-model tables tilt 45 degrees right, and from zero to up to 15 degrees left (the bottom wheel interferes with left tilt on band saws).

There are so many band saws in various sizes, that you can find something to match just about any budget. Twelve-inch saws tend to cost in the $350 to $500 range. Most 14" floor model band saws are in the $400 to $700 range, although it's possible to spend twice that. Larger band saws cost more, as you'd expect, although you can find some 15" models for around $300. Good ballpark figures for a basic 15" model is $500 to $600, then add a 100 bucks every time you go up an inch. It's possible, of course, to pay far more to get better fit and finish, more power, longer warranty, a certain brand name and other features. But don't go too big. Generally an 18" model is about the top size needed for a recreational or small "pro" shop.

Beyond a 14" floor-model band saw, higher-end band saws, such as the Laguna line (above), offer increased power and up to 24" resaw capacity.

In Floor Models, Look For:

- Sturdy frame of cast iron or steel.
- Rigidity is essential for maintaining blade tension and reducing vibration, so cast iron is best, but thick sheet-steel also works well.
- Smoothly milled table, with a fine finish.
- At least an 8- to 12-amp ¾-hp motor. Check that the horsepower is appropriate to the amperage (about 8 to 12 amps for a ¾-hp motor; 10 to 15 amps for 1 hp). If it's not, then the manufacturer is exaggerating the saw's power.
- Easy dust collection port hook-up.
- Cleanly cast metal blade wheels.
- Easy-to-adjust blade guide controls.
- Roller-bearing blade guides.
- Easy-opening doors for blade access.
- A table that locks rigidly into place. Is there left-tilt on the table of at least 10 degrees, and how easily does the tilt mechanism work?
- Sufficient cutting capacity for your needs. Is a riser kit available?

The Coin Flip:

Unless space is at a premium, you can't go wrong selecting a 14" to 16" two-wheel floor model band saw. Make sure you get at least a 1 hp motor, more if you've got a lot of resawing in your plans. Most band saws run on 110-volt circuits, and some can be changed to use 220, but usually there's not much advantage to doing this. The greater your resawing needs, however, the more horsepower you need, and the more likely you are to need a 220-volt circuit.

If space is limited and it's got to fit on a bench, buy as much quality (i.e., a brand name you trust) and power as your budget allows. Don't sacrifice cutting ability or stock capacity. Aim for ⅓- to ½-hp motors in either two- or three-wheel designs.

The critical decision points come down to price, brand name if that's important to you, easily reached and operated adjustments, adequate power for your intended use and desire. If you don't mind messing with machinery,

BUZZ WORDS

Horsepower
Too many advertised electric-motor horsepower ratings are victims of gross exaggeration. Usually listed is the "peak" horsepower, which only exists when the motor first starts up. If this is the figure you see, knock about 25 percent off the claimed hp to get your real working "oomph." Check also that the amp rating matches the horsepower claims. For a ¾-hp motor, the amp range should be 8 to 12 amps; for 1 hp and above, it should be 10 to 15 amps.

TEFC (totally enclosed fan-cooled motor)
This is a nice touch that adds to motor durability, but is more costly. Depending on how hard you use and abuse the saw, you may never notice any difference. Regular motors work well and last a long time if blown clean occasionally.

Left tilt of at least 5 degrees
Great to have if you do much dovetailing with your band saw, but that's pretty much all it's used for.

Wheel size
Size does matter, but only if you've got the motor to spin those big wheels. The bigger the wheels, the more powerful the motor must be, plus it needs a sturdier, heavier stand, a bigger frame, a larger table, etc. Don't obsess about size. Bigger saws are nice, but they're more expensive to buy and run, blades cost more and can be harder to find, and accessories are not as common.

you can save some money by getting a more roughly finished band saw that takes longer to setup.

Band saws are more important in the woodshop than many people realize, which is one reason there are over 100 models and brands out there. So expect to take the time to shop around, ponder the tiny print in "spec" charts, twiddle with the adjustments in the store and otherwise "kick the tires" before making your purchasing decision.

Other Good Stuff For Band Saws

Buy good blades. A band saw that has problems with a standard cheap blade can improve an amazing amount when you wrap a good blade around its wheels. You may pay as much as 150 percent more, but the speed and quality of the cut makes it well worth the expense.

Invest in better blade guidance. Your choices are either synthetic-guide block systems such as Cool Block, a graphite-impregnated phenolic laminate plastic, or ball bearing guides. The Carter Guide is a well-respected bearing guide that can tremendously improve your band saw's performance.

The Carter Guides are expensive at about $150, while the Cool Blocks and its imitators are about $15 for a pack of four (upper and lower) guides. Roller guides for side thrust fit inside the present guide holders cost about $70.

Riser kits increase the resawing capacity of band saws and are available for most 14" saws and some other sizes. If making big resaws is in your plans, even occasionally, check the availability of a riser kit before you buy the saw. Don't wait until afterward to see if one is offered. Riser kits will cost from about $60 to $100 depending on the brand. The kits start with the riser block, a block of cast iron in the same cross-section as the neck of the band saw. It fits into holes and locating pins on the current assembly and bolts in place. You'll also get longer blade guards, and most kits include a new, longer blade. Installation is usually easy.

Get better rip fences and miter gauges, with the miter gauge the more important choice. Optional rip fences are usually in the $15 to $30 range, while a good miter gauge may cost from $30 to $60.

biscuit joiners

Biscuit joiners (also called plate joiners) came to the United States about a decade ago, after becoming popular in Europe. They immediately found a following here. Instead of dowels at joints, flat football-shaped biscuits made of compressed wood fibers slip into slots cut by the biscuit joiner. Glue is added into in the slots and along the edge being joined for a very tough joint. It sounds and looks oddball, but the result is a tight, strong joint that is exceptionally easy to true up — far easier than aligning a dowel joint, regardless of joint position.

Using biscuits with T, butt or mitered joints is as easy as it is for flat joints. Biscuit joiners also cut special half-football-shaped mortises for specialized cabinet hinges that can both speed up cabinet work and add a different look to the finished project.

What's Out There

The biscuit joiner is a one-trick pony. A joiner is a simple cutting tool with a fence that presses against the work surface, and a spring-loaded motor body with a 4" six- or eight-tooth blade. The blade is set to cut to one of three specific depths to fit specific biscuit sizes (0, the smallest standard size, which is

Porter-Cable's model 557 biscuit joiner has both 2"- and 4"-diameter blades for standard or face-frame biscuits.

47 mm long; 10, 52 mm long; and 20, 58 mm long). Standard biscuit width varies from 14 mm to 24 mm. There is a blade change for some biscuit joiners that bring sizes down to the FF (face frame), a 13 mm-wide by 30 mm-long biscuit, which works out a great deal better for face frames and similar constructs where project width isn't great enough to accept regular biscuits.

A 4"-long Max biscuit is also available. The extra-width biscuit is handy in projects where thick or long sections are joined. The Max biscuit requires cutting longer slots, which is done by making two cuts that overlap one another. For these biscuits, a joiner with an extra-depth adjustment and specially marked fence makes things easier.

Understanding the Features

The biggest claim biscuit joiners can stake is that they replace dowel and mortise-and-tenon joinery. In many cases, that's the absolute truth, with special emphasis on dowel joinery. The mortise-and-tenon replacement claim is OK in some instances, but "iffy" in others. The extra strength provided by a good mortise-and-tenon joint should not always be sacrificed to the great speed of biscuit installation (such as in chair construction), but it is a case-by-case decision.

In some instances, substitution is not possible: Biscuits don't work in material less than 1½" in width, even with the newer small sizes, because of the shape of the cutout.

Claims of power are meaningful only to a point. If you're not turning out hundreds of cuts a day, lower power (and cost) is just fine. Top-of-the-line production tools are great, too, but not necessary for most of us. Do you really need to spend $400 for a one-job tool when a cost of $100 to $200 will fulfill all you need? Think it over.

Look for a truly ergonomic handle (that means one that feels comfortable

---

HANDY JIG

Possibly the handiest jig for the biscuit joiner is only a piece of plywood or MDF, sized to fit your needs (at least 18" x 20"). Align a straight 1x3 board along its back edge, with one edge flush to the plywood edge. That forms a back-edge stop for cutting biscuit slots in the sides of boards. Just clamp the jig to a benchtop, insert the board you need to slot and cut the slots on the marks.

To add right-angle capability to the jig, move in a few inches from one end, and screw down another 1x3 at an exact right angle to the first 1x3, but leaving a 6" gap between the two boards. This allows cutting slots in right-angle material, and sets a width limit of 6" on material width for Tees and other face frame structures. You make the gap smaller or larger as needed for different jigs.

---

to your, and not someone else's, paw). Check out dust collection. That's a need, not an option. Are you doing face frames? Right now, only a couple of brands offer a smaller blade size to handle shorter biscuits that work in narrow stock. The fence may have an immense range of degree settings, or it may have more positive detents. One fence sets from 0 to 135 degrees (which is needed to allow inside and outside 45 degree use), but has a positive detent only at 90 degrees. Another sets at 0 to 90 degrees, with detents at those two ends, of course, and at 45 degrees. Others set positively in different ways, and also work to 135 degrees. Decide which you need most. Check out adjustment features and, if you can, check the kinds of knobs used. Some are more easily adjusted than others.

Power

Most joiners are in the 5- to 7½-amp power range and, since cuts are shallow and short, more power simply isn't needed. The extra power offered by some models makes cuts slightly faster, but also gives you a motor that's more durable because it's never stressed to the utmost. Whether you need that extra bit of durability depends on how heavily your joiner will be used. The motors are universal, a little noisy but very powerful for their size and weight, and brush changes are possible. Most biscuit joiners operate at about 10,000 rpm.

Fences

Unlike with most power tools, for which different power levels define their abilities, with biscuit joiners it's the fence that's most important. This is the big variable and your preference here is what's most important. Fences need to operate smoothly and easily, lock in tightly and be accurate. If they're also simple to use, that's a major bonus.

Most fences have stops at 0, 45 and 90 degrees, but also can be set at any angle in between for exact fits (some fences do not allow more than the three settings, which are enough for

most purposes). A number of fences work to 135 degrees, and one works to 180 degrees. This allows for inside and outside work without taking the fence off and turning it around.

Joiners can be used, and used well, without fences. But, good fences make it easier for you to do good work, to reduce surface finishing needs when joining wide panels and to get accurate miter, and other joints that are strongly braced, joined.

Depth Stops

The depth stop is a part of the biscuit joiner that must also be excellent. Its accuracy is possibly more important than that of the fence, because you can adapt to a slightly "off" fence, but if you're drilling holes too deep, or not deep enough, the biscuits simply will not fit. The standard three biscuit sizes each need a different depth. Then there are smaller biscuit sizes, cut with a 2" accessory blade that require even more adjustments and, finally, the Max biscuit needs a greater depth. Standard biscuit joiners may have just three depth adjustments. Better models will have as many as seven.

Dust Collection

Most biscuit joiners offer a dust collection bag. Though reasonably efficient, they fill up quickly. You may want to check on the many adapters for the various diameters that are available so that vacuums may be connected for better lung protection when you're cutting a lot of slots.

Small Joiners

There are a couple of small biscuit joiners on the market at very low cost. Their weights are under 4 pounds, draw is less than four amperes, and no-load motor speed is 20,000 rpm. The fences have the same three primary settings (0, 45 and 90 degrees) that other fences have, but the entire joiner is made small. This is made possible with the use of a smaller blade and motor, letting the tool use biscuits that are about half the size of the smallest standard biscuits. These small joiners are great for medium-duty use in constructing small projects and work well with picture frames, as well as face frames on small cabinets.

Pricing

You'll find biscuit joiners selling for a mere $50 for the small machines using miniature biscuits, with "pro" production models of the tools rising to about $700. One stationary model is available, about in the mid-range of those costs. Joiners that cut slots only for the smallest biscuit sizes are available for around $50, while standard biscuit joiners kick in a little higher. Evaluate your uses, and see just what you expect most to do, and how much of it. There is a good selection in the middle price ranges, from about $130 to $200. Spending more than $200 is probably a waste for the small shop.

In Biscuit Joiners, Look For:

- Overall lightness. The lighter the biscuit joiner is, the easier it is to use, short of being so light it is poorly made.
- Is the fence comprehensive enough for your uses? At least one model has a 180-degree range, while several work to 135 degrees. Is the fence easy to set at any of its positions? Does it lock tightly?
- Does it have positive stops at enough angles? Three is the usual: 0, 45 and 90 degrees.
- Does the depth stop work easily?
- Is the depth stop accurate?
- Can you adjust the depth stop easily?
- Does it adapt to cutting smaller or larger biscuit slots? Do you need it to?
- How powerful is it? The range is 3.5 to 7.5 amperes, for handheld models, while the benchtop is 10 amperes.
- Is the switch easy to reach?
- Does the switch lock on for production work?
- How loud is it? Gear-driven joiners are louder than belt-driven. This is very important if you use it for long periods of time.

BISCUITS

Biscuits, regardless of size, are compressed birch fibers. Currently, the range of sizes is as wide as it has ever been, with the basic 0, 10 and 20 (reading small to large). Below 0, you can now find FF (face frame) biscuits, with slots cut by a 2" blade. And below that are the two mini-biscuit joiners, with R1, R2 and R3 biscuits for smaller projects. These tiny biscuits are superb for miters in small boxes and similar areas. When a biscuit gets too close to the thickness of the wood, being joined, there is a chance that as it absorbs water and time passes, you'll get a print-through of the biscuit shape in the wood. Smaller biscuits reduce print-through chances. The Max biscuits can be installed in cuts made with almost any biscuit joiner, but joiners with specially marked fences for these long fellows are easiest to use. If you plan on building up benchtops or countertops out of solid wood, give some thought to this size.

To save money, buy your biscuits in packs of 1000 (a bag of 1000 assorted 0, 10, 20 costs about $20 plus shipping. FF biscuits are about $8 a tube of 175), depending on your anticipated needs. Unless you're doing production work, buying more is not a good idea because biscuits can absorb water from the surrounding air, swell, and become difficult or impossible to fit.

Keep biscuits in a dry environment. When you open the pack, transfer the unused biscuits immediately to a Zip-loc or similar bag. Keep them cool, dry and tightly sealed and they'll stay useful.

The Coin Flip:

With biscuit joiners, your choice is usually limited to one model from each manufacturer (with a couple of exceptions). Several will be totally unsuited in price to small shops. The rest are almost all capable of doing the work, with varying degrees of ease and versatility. Select the biscuit joiner that covers the largest number of biscuit sizes in the ranges you need. You need a joiner with five or more amperes for full-size work, and at least 3.5 amperes for work with compact biscuits. Joiners with cords at least 10' long keep you from spending your time worrying about hanging up an extension cord on boards or bench edges.

Where does the dust bag fall? Most are just fine where they are, but some may get in the way of movement in and around workpieces. Check. What bothers one person isn't even noticed by another, so see how it works for you.

Lamello Top 20 biscuit joiner, one of the best-selling models.

When it comes to portable drills, you're actually looking at two types of products. A corded electric tool used most often as just a drill, and cordless drill/drivers which are used as either a drill or as a power screwdriver. While you can use a cordless drill/driver for most applications, there are still situations where a corded drill is the best option. When drilling with larger spade, Forstner or auger bits, it's less efficient to use a cordless drill. Though battery performance and torque in cordless drills continues to improve, it's unlikely you'll see a match for the raw power of a corded drill anytime soon, and it's very difficult to beat the run-time of a wall outlet. On the other hand, the flexibility, finesse and convenience of a cordless drill/driver is something no one will want to give up once they've experienced it. Our answer is to own a corded drill (which is usually pretty affordable), as well as a cordless drill/driver (or three).

When it comes to ultimate power without interruption, corded drills such as Milwaukee's ½" model 0235-20 still reign.

Battery chargers can show you much more than just the status of your battery's charge; it can also help diagnose problems with the battery.

BATTERIES

Here's a fun bit of information: There are only three companies making batteries for all the cordless tools for sale in the U.S. today. Battery technology is pretty "niche" stuff, and expecting all the tool manufacturers to be producing their own technology isn't realistic. Batteries, in general, are very basic animals.

They are a collection of 1.3- or 1.7-amp cells arranged inside the battery case itself. By adding more cells to the battery, the voltage is increased and, as you've noticed, the larger the voltage on a tool, the larger and heavier the battery. Not all cells are exactly the same. The one obvious difference is what the battery is made from. The industry standard is a cell based on Nickel Cadmium (NiCad) as the "medium." Seeing some growth in the industry is the Nickel Metal Hydride (NiMH) battery which has been standard in electronic appliances, such as cell phones and computers, for a number of years.

The NiMH batteries are designed to hold a longer charge in a small space and the NiMH battery cell offers more run time in the same size cell. So, you may ask: "Is the battery in my Makita drill the same as in my Panasonic drill?" While the two batteries may actually be made by the same battery manufacturer, the cell composition can be different, providing different life expectancies and performance. So the answer is "no." Not all batteries are created equal, even by the same creator.

One question we've been asked a few times is: Why are replacement batteries so expensive? While a new 12-volt cordless drill with two batteries may cost $140, a single replacement battery can cost $50 or more. Does this mean the rest of the drill is only worth $40? No, what you are seeing here is the law of supply and demand. Your tool store is a part of a very competitive market and every manufacturer has to work on a pretty tight profit margin to get their tools on the shelf - if it's a cordless drill. The spare batteries, on the other hand, don't fall into that competitive category and are often a special-order item. While, yes, the cells used to make the batteries are somewhat expensive, it's the competitive tool market that makes the drill kit cheap, while the spare batteries reflect a more realistic price. So, rather than feeling that you're being taken advantage of, appreciate the competitive market that allows you to buy the original tool (with two batteries) at such a great price. And, besides, with today's performance technology, it's much less likely you'll need a spare battery.

Understanding the Features

While there are differences between corded and cordless models, there are some similar features that you should be familiar with, no matter which type you're in the market for.

Chuck Capacity and Type

A simple option to consider is whether the drill's chuck is a ⅜" or ½" capacity. While nine times out of 10 a ⅜" chuck opening will be sufficient, if you're buying a corded drill for it's extreme bit capacity and raw performance, the ½" chuck capacity may be your obvious better option. While considering the chuck, also consider a keyless or keyed chuck option. One of the best tool innovations of the last 10 years, the keyless chuck allows tool-free changing of bits, saving time and sanity. That said, many of the ½"-chuck drills available on the market are still only available with a keyed chuck. They're not being mean. The manufacturer's rationale (and we tend to agree) is that if you are chucking a foot-long 1⅛"-diameter auger bit into a drill, you don't want it slipping. While keyless chucks improve every day, the available pressure is still better on a keyed chuck. So look to your needs to determine which chuck feature is most important to you.

VSR (Variable Speed Reversing)

In our opinion, variable speed reversing makes a drill able to perform raw power requirements, as well as handle tasks requiring finesse. By lightly touching the trigger, the revolution speed of the drill bit (or screw bit) can be controlled with great accuracy to allow the bit to perform at its optimum level. More than a feature, we wouldn't buy a drill that wasn't VSR capable.

Corded Drills

While one of the most basic woodworking tools, there are still a wide variety of choices available. Corded drills run from $29 models to $229. In general, we tend to think around $75 is plenty and $50 is likely adequate.

Extension Cords Wire Size

Cord Length	AMP Rating of Tool (Full Load)					
	0-2.0	2.1-3.4	3.5-5.0	5.1-7.0	7.1-12.0	12.1-16.0
25	18	18	18	18	16	14
50	18	18	18	16	14	12
75	18	18	16	14	12	10
100	18	16	14	12	10	8
150	16	14	12	10	8	8
200	16	14	12	10	8	6
300	14	12	10	8	6	4
400	12	10	8	6	4	4
500	12	10	8	6	4	2
600	10	8	6	4	2	2
800	10	8	6	4	2	1
1000	8	6	4	2	1	0

NOTE: This table is for 115V tools.

The Cord

Don't overlook the thing that makes a corded drill desirable. While it provides unlimited run-time and amazing torque, it doesn't have to limit your range of motion. Drill cords come in many lengths, with many of the European models offering a 20-foot cord. Why not have the best of corded and cordless?

In Corded Drills, Look For:

- VSR. If it doesn't have it, buy better.
- ½" chuck. You'll benefit from the extra power.
- Cord length. A longer (rubber, not plastic) cord is better.
- Chucks. Keyed or keyless chuck; let your conscience guide you.
- Feel. More than any other power tool, how it fits in your hand is very important in a corded drill.

EXTENSION CORDS

Don't take extension cords for granted. Most electrical fires start in extension cords, and the voltage drain can affect the performance of your tool — or stop it altogether. For instance, take Dave Thiel, *Popular Woodworking* magazine's senior editor. He bought a 20-gallon compressor and was going to nail together a shed in his backyard. So, he ran his trusty orange extension cord from the garage outlet to the backyard, plugged the compressor in and flipped the switch. Nothing. He tried a few more times and, still, "no go."

When he plugged a drill into the same cord, he had no power — blown breaker. Simple to diagnose ... he'd had it on a 15-amp breaker and compressors are amp pigs. Dave changed to a 20-amp breaker and tried again. This time the compressor chugged, then tripped the breaker on the compressor. Seems the extension cord was only rated for 15 amps. Not to mention, he had it stretched to its full 150-foot length.

Buy an extension cord rated to the job you are likely to use it for. And when you can't find a 20-amp extension cord long enough for what you want to do, take another lesson. As current travels, there is a voltage drop over the line and, if the cord is too long, the voltage drop will make the current inefficient to perform the required task. So move closer to the power source, or think about a generator.

In general, the chart (above left) will help you choose the best cord for your needs.

While all batteries work on similar cell designs, how the pack itself mates to the drill widely varies.

Cordless Drills/Drivers

In addition to the benefits (and drawbacks) mentioned above, cordless drill/drivers are the purview of the chuck clutch. In addition to the finesse made available by variable speed control, a clutch allows the user to set the torque to release — to avoid over-setting of screws, or stripping the head off a screw.

Volts, Amp Hours and Chargers

Cordless drill/drivers are rated by performance into voltage categories, ranging from 7.2 volts (or less) to 24 volts (the maximum for now). In comparing same-volt drill/drivers, the number of amp hours the battery offers should also be considered. To put it in very simplistic terms, think of the voltage of the tool as the motor size of an engine. More volts, more horsepower. The amp hour rating is like the gas tank. The higher the amp hour rating, the larger the gas tank. So if you have the option of a 12-volt drill with either a 1.7-amp hour battery or a 2-amp hour battery, they'll both drill the same — but the 2-amp hour drill will drill longer at that level. Another battery-related feature option is the speed of the charger. The norm is a one-hour charger, an attractive upgrade is a 15-minute charger, but with most drill/drivers including two batteries, a 15-minute charger may be a luxury not worth paying for. On the other hand, unless a very basic and low-use drill/driver is what your needs require, a three-hour charger can be a drawback on some tools.

The Clutch

Many cordless drills offer an adjustable clutch. While we consider this a desirable feature, we are a little puzzled by the inclusion of up to 24 clutch positions on some models. While certainly offering a wide range of finesse, we tend to think three or five positions should be more than adequate.

High/Low Speed

Another feature unique to cordless drills is the option of high or low speed. This is more than a function of slowing down the drill/driver speed. The low-speed setting is designed for maximum torque production, most beneficial when using the tool as a screwdriver. The high-speed setting is designed for producing the appropriate speed (or as close as possible) for the optimum performance of drill bits. Buy a drill with two speed settings, and learn to use those settings as designed.

Milwaukee's battery, shown here, can be reversed to change the balance of the gun for overhead work.

Hopefully you won't ever have to see the inside of your drill, but if you did, this is what you'd find.

Type of Handle

Cordless drills are available in T- or center-handled design, or pistol-grip, with the handle to the rear of the tool. While pistol-grip drills are still favored for continuous quick screw placement, the T-handle is the best all-around design. Pistol grips allow the user to provide force directly inline with the screw or drill axis more easily. T-handles provide much better balance, and allow the tool to stand upright when not in use.

Kits

Many manufacturers are offering their cordless drill drivers in kits, including at least an extra battery and case and, at most, four different tools using the same battery platform. While two batteries are a great idea and a true asset, be cautious about getting sucked into buying more than you need because it's a bargain. Good bargains do include adding a flashlight or power screwdriver for almost the same price.

In Cordless Drills, Look For:

- VSR. You must have it in a cordless drill.
- Keyless chuck. A ⅜" keyless chuck is best all-around.
- Clutch. Get one with four or more positions.
- Volts/amps. Get the right amount for your needs.
- Handle. Get a T-handle or pistol-grip handle; we prefer the T-handle.
- Speed. Should have high/low speed for best performance.
- Two batteries.

The Coin Flip:

As mentioned earlier, our suggestion is to purchase a corded drill (of moderate price) for heavy or highly repeatable tasks. Add a 9.6-volt or 12-volt cordless drill (or both) to this for more precise woodworking applications. Get two batteries, variable speed and high/low, and a keyless ⅜" chuck. If you feel the need for more power in a cordless, look to 14.4- or 18-volt drills as a maximum.

Two-sleeve keyless chuck

High/low rpm switch

Variable clutch

Forward and reverse switch

T-handle with soft grip

Porter-Cable cordless drill, model number 9866.

DeWalt's drill package, shown here, includes drill, jigsaw and battery pack.

Why You Want One

Your shop can't survive without a drill press if you're drilling more than a few holes — and what project doesn't require that? A drill press gives you greater accuracy with any type of hole drilling, and that usually translates into faster work when you've got multiple holes to bore. (Simple jigs can really increase work speed with multiple holes.) "Walking" (when the bit-point moves out of the hole) is a thing of the past with a drill press. Neat, clean holes become the rule rather than the exception. Even the steadiest hands and the best bit in a handheld portable drill won't match the results you'll get from even the cheapest drill press.

Drill presses also offer the opportunity to use circle cutters, large Forstner bits and other bits that don't work well, if at all, in handheld drills. Floor models and benchtop models offer the same flexibility for using a variety of cutters, but the floor models offer greater drilling depth.

Understanding the Features

Depth Stops

Depth stops take the risk out of gauging your accuracy while drilling partway through boards. You control exactly how far down the bit travels. Set it up correctly once, and drill all the holes you need at that setting with no fuss or strain. Depth stops are also great for drilling shelf supports in book cases and cabinets.

Lots of Speeds

Drill bit speeds are meant to be — or should be — easily adjustable by moving belts on multiple pulleys. You swap belts from one groove to another in order to vary speeds from as low as 150 rpm on some drills to as high as 3000 rpm. A couple of drill presses offer continuously adjustable speeds — a nice feature. Slow speeds are ideal for larger Forstner bits and circle cutters, while faster speeds make quick work of smaller holes.

Quill Travel

Quill travel is a very important feature. It determines how far the bit can penetrate. In every case, longer is better because it means easy drilling of deep holes. Quill travel varies from as little as 2" in many benchtop drill presses, to as much as 6" in pricey upper-bracket styles. Quill travel in a good floor-model machine should be between 3¼" and 4", which is fine for most situations you're likely to encounter.

Horsepower

The horsepower-exaggeration race hasn't hit the small shop drill press as hard as it has hit other tool categories. Benchtop drill presses range from a mere ¼ horsepower, to as much as ¾ hp. Floor models will range from 1/2 to perhaps 1½ hp. Oddly, the costly drill presses give value in other areas, usually claiming no more than a 1 hp.

Capacities

Drill presses get their size designations based on the distance from the center of the drill bit chuck to the column behind it. Thus, if you buy a drill press with 6" from the chuck's center to the column, you have a 12" tool because it

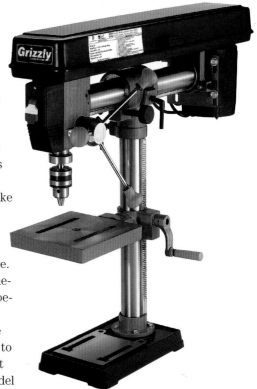

Grizzly's G7945 benchtop radial drill press.

will drill to the center of a 12" circle. The actual working capacity, however, is more a function of chuck size and motor power. The drill chucks on smaller floor models are ½" or ⅝". Larger models will have ¾" chucks.

General hobby and small shops are best equipped with floor models in the 15- to 17" capacity, with a ½" or ⅝" chuck. Such drill presses are reasonable in price and often have as many as 16 speeds, down to a low of 150 rpm (ideal for large Forstner bits, which burn up quickly at high speeds) and as high as 3600 twists per minute. The cost for most such tools kicks in around $500, give or take 50 bucks. Unless your projects have exceptional needs, this is a good all-around size.

What's Out There

The drill press world is well stocked. Benchtop models with capacities to 14" are available, as are those with 8" capacities. Prices range from as little as $80 to as much as $280. Standard floor models have capacities ranging from 13½" to as much as 20½" with costs rising pretty much in line with features, from a low of under $200 to over $1000. Radial bench presses have capacities as low as 13" and as much as 36", with prices from $180 to about $500.

Prices vary depending on power, features such as number of speeds, and chuck size.

Benchtop Drill Presses

For light-duty and small project use, benchtop drill presses can be ideal. Sizes (throat capacities) range from 8" to 14", with other models at 10", 12" and 13".

Quill travel (the depth you can drill in a single pass) is limited, with a low of 2" and a top of 3½". Low speeds range from a very low 140 rpm in a couple of models, to 700 rpm in one, and 620 in many others (faster is less desirable unless you never expect to use Forstner bits). Top end speeds range from 3000 to 4910 rpm.

Most benchtop brands have fewer speeds available than do floor models, and horsepower is limited. The lowest horsepower available is ¼, with a peak of ¾. Several features are less likely to be available, so deciding on the need for them is important. Tilt tables are available on only a very few benchtop drill presses, and about half do not have rack-and-pinion table height adjustment. Most have ½" chucks, though several offer ⅝" chucks.

Two table styles are generally available. One, usually round, has oil grooves and can be used for metal work, as well as wood (these grooves can take special clamps). The second, usually rectangular, has pierced slots for regular woodworking clamps. This may also be used for metal, but there are no grooves to trap oil.

Skil benchtop drill press.

In Benchtop Drill Presses, Look For:

- Controls up front (on-off switch, automatic speed control, if any).
- Chuck capacity and quality — does it adjust and lock easily?
- Easy travel of quill, both up and down.
- Easy-to-use depth stop.
- Throat capacity.

Tip *When you can't afford fancy freestanding or benchtop sanders, a set of rubber sanding drums, with sanding sleeves, can be chucked in a drill press to make short work of shaping and of finishing inside curves. A set of drums with a few sleeves in varied grits can be bought for under $25.*

- Number of speeds.
- Lowest speed (slower is better if you use Forstner bits, circle cutters, similar accessories).
- Post rigidity, general solidity.
- An easily lifted top for belt changes (latches easily, lifts easily, re-latches easily).
- Ease of movement of table.
- Table tilt.
- Security of table locks — does it lock in position vertically? Does tilt lock easily?
- Table size and type.
- Ease of up and down movement of table on column —rack-and-pinion is easiest.
- Presence or absence of work light.

Floor-Model Drill Presses

The floor-model drill press is the ultimate in small-shop drill presses. If shop floor space and budget allow, these heavyweights (some weigh almost 350 pounds, others are lighter, about 125 pounds) present the greatest basic throat and chuck capacities, largest number of speeds, longest quill travel, most horsepower, greatest table travel vertically and largest work tables.

Speeds

Floor drill press speeds range from a truly ambling low of 150 rpm to a high of 4200. The general range is 250 to 3300. Slower is better for larger drills and cutters, with large Forstner bits (over 2") demanding speeds from 450 rpm down as speed increases. Higher speeds work better with other types of bits and other applications. The usual floor model has three pulleys with several sized grooves on each. There will be

JET's model JDP-17MFW 16½" drill press.

two belts, changed from pulley to pulley to reduce or increase speed. The floor models have from 12 to 16 speeds.

Quill Travel

Quill travel is as important with floor-model drill presses as it is with benchtops — and longer is better. Floor drill presses offer generally deeper drilling possibilities, with the shortest quill travel at 3", compared to the 2" short end of benchtop models, to a lengthy 6". Most common is the 3¼" to 4⅞" range.

Depth Stops

Depth stops are very handy in repetitive drilling situations (bookshelf sides for supports, among other chores). Some stops are much easier to use than others. The threaded rod-and-nut style (two nuts, one locking the other in place) is fast to adjust. Another option is a collar-locking device attached to the handle spindle. Both have advantages and are a personal preference.

Tables

Tables on floor-model drill presses are larger than those on benchtop models, sometimes twice as large. There are round and rectangular types, and oil-groove and through-slot types, with the oil groove based on metalworking needs, and through slot types aimed directly at woodworkers. Either type works, but clamping is easier with through slots. Table size is important — the bigger, the better, regardless of style.

Table raising systems don't vary much. There is the bare post, with main force being the methodm and the rack-and-pinion system with a handle to crank the table up or down. Rack-and-pinion wins unless cost is important.

Table tilt can be important for some projects, and having a tilting table sometimes saves you having to build a tilt jig.

Weight

Stationary woodworking tools benefit from heavy castings, the heavier, the better. Floor drill presses are no exception. If the model you like is lightweight, make sure it has holes for easily bolting to the floor. Drill presses that weigh a

lot may not need direct floor attachment. The heavier weight absorbs vibration, making the tool operate more smoothly (all else — such as quill, arbor and chuck run-out, pulley balance, belt type, tightness of belts, solidity of motor mounting — are equal). Smoother operation equals more accurate drilling.

Power and Motors

The low-end power on floor drill presses is ½ hp. The high end is 1½ hp. For almost all woodworking, ¾ hp on a ⅝" chuck is easily sufficient. Totally enclosed fan-cooled (TEFC) motors are generally more durable. Non-TEFC motors are reasonably durable and cut costs, sometimes considerably.

In Floor-Model Drill Presses, Look For:

- Up-front controls (on-off switch, automatic speed control, if any).
- Chuck capacity and quality — does chuck suit your needs, does it adjust and lock easily?
- Quill travel length. Easy travel of quill, both up and down.
- Easy-to-use depth stop.
- Throat capacity.
- Number of speeds (at least 12).
- Lowest speed (slower is better if you use Forstner bits, circle cutters, similar accessories).
- Post rigidity, general solidity, weight of base.
- An easily lifted top for belt changes (latches easily, lifts easily, re-latches easily).
- Ease of movement of table, even without a rack-and-pinion crank, but rack-and-pinion is easiest.
- Table tilt — how much does it tilt, how easy does it tilt?
- Security of table locks — does it lock solidly in position vertically, does tilt lock easily.
- Table size and type.
- Power and motor type (TEFC or non-TEFC).
- Weight.
- Presence or absence of worklight.
- Good fit and finish overall — especially on the pulleys, chuck, arbor and quill.

Radial Drill Presses

The radial drill press is the poor person's answer to huge capacity industrial drill presses. If you often need to drill to the center of a 22" or larger workpiece, your only reasonably priced alternative is the radial drill press. These are available in benchtop and floor models, with capacities from 26" to 36", and either ½" chucks (benchtop models) or ⅝" chucks (one benchtop, the rest floor models). Horsepower ranges from a low of ¼ to a high of ½.

Radial drill presses have a pull-out drill head radial tube set-up that adds to capacity. Capacities on most small radial drill presses are greater than 24", and some are considerably more, up to 36". The downside of radial drill presses is the probability of deflection in the radial shaft, which reduces accuracy of drilling. The upside is the fact that deflection can usually be limited by careful use, and the low price of an otherwise industrial-grade capacity drill press. When you need to work to the center of wide panels, radial drill presses do the job well, at moderate cost.

Ultimate Capacity

While radial drill presses can give you the capacity of an industrial drill press costing thousands of dollars, for $500 and less (to about $150), they present one problem massive industrial drills don't. The long horizontal shaft is easily flexed if any sideways forces are brought to bear when moving the quill down to drill. Thus accuracy can be a problem, though the use of care when bringing the quill down helps reduce problems. So does careful set-up and general careful handling of the machine.

Features on radial drill presses are similar to those on floor and benchtop models with solid heads. The speed selection range may be smaller, and weight is always less (the heaviest radial drill press weighs just over 150 pounds), but speed adjustments are made with belts and pulleys, depth stops are the same or similar, tables tilt, and work lights may be available.

Ryobi's **WDP1850** is a drill press designed for woodworkers. The adjustable table (above) includes an adjustable fence and hold-down clamp.

Another feature of Ryobi's drill press is the speed adjustment during operation; no messing with belts and pulleys.

MORTISING ATTACHMENT

Mortising attachments are great ways to power your way through a sometimes tedious-to-make joint part. A fence attaches to the drill press table and a guide/chisel/drill bit combination fits on the quill, and in the chuck. Set at modest speed (around 1400–1800 rpm), the chisel and bit cut a clean square hole to a pre-set depth. Cut several and you've got a mortise. Shaping a tenon to fit can be done with any saw. Cost is generally under $100, often under $80.

Head Tilting

One additional feature is available with radial drill presses. Most have tilting heads. The tilting head combines with a tilting table to create a dizzying range of possible hole drilling angles. Head tilts are usually 90 degrees left, and 45 or 50 degrees right, but a couple of models reverse this and give the biggest tilt to the right.

In Radial Drill Presses, Look For:

- Up-front controls (on-off switch, automatic speed control, if any).
- Chuck capacity and quality — does chuck suit your needs? Does it adjust and lock easily?
- Ease of quill travel.
- Quill travel distance.
- Easy-to-use depth stop.
- Throat capacity — this is the radial drill press's shining feature, up to three full feet.
- Number of speeds.
- Lowest speed (slower is better with many accessories). Most radial drill presses have a fairly high low speed (550–620), but several do offer 250 or 310 rpm.
- Head rigidity, ease of adjustment in and out (some use rack-and-pinion here, as well as on the main column).
- Head tilt, right and left.
- An easily operated top for belt changes.
- Ease of movement of table.

- Table tilt — how much, how easy and in which directions?
- Security of table locks — does it lock solidly in position vertically?
- Table size and type.
- Power and motor type (TEFC or non-TEFC).

The Coin Flip:

A drill press may be really important in your shop, and will become more so as time goes on. It is a versatile tool that easily uses any accessory available for handheld drills, many types and sizes of drill bits and hole saws, metalworking accessories such as milling tables, and it provides great accuracy in diameter and depth hole drilling with any kind of drill bit.

The choice you make depends on a number of factors, starting with any brand and price range. From there, select for the amount and type of use you expect to give the drill press. If you do a lot of metalworking as well as woodworking, get a drill press that has oil grooves in its table. If you do mostly woodworking, with only an occasional foray into metal drilling, then select a woodworking table with its through slots to ease the installation of jigs and the holding of workpieces.

Select the power you need or expect to need, and match the chuck size to the power. A ½-" chuck works fine with ¼-hp to ½-hp motors. ⅝" and ¾" chucks demand at least ¾ hp. Deep drilling needs more power — if you do lamp building, or other turnings that might require holes over 3" or 4" deep, then select for more power and a greater speed selection.

The more kinds of materials you drill, the more speeds you will find useful. Metal, wood and plastic all require different speeds. More speed variations are added by the type and size of drill bits used. Metal milling takes different speeds, depending on the metal

and the type and size of the mill.

Select the throat capacity you need.

If shop space is limited, select a benchtop model that can be easily lifted down and stored when not in use — or pushed aside and stored.

You'll find about 60 drill presses in sizes that are useful in the hobby and small "pro" shop, costing under $1000. The most likely winners are in a range of $450 to $575, and may offer the best values of capacity, accuracy, durability, and utility.

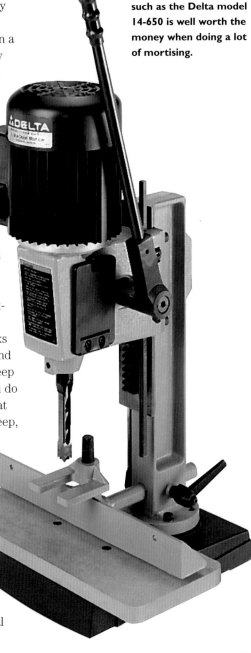

A dedicated mortiser such as the Delta model 14-650 is well worth the money when doing a lot of mortising.

Craftsman 16-gallon convertible vacuum, model 17016.

Dust collection is an important part of any woodworking shop. In recent years, the recognition of wood dust as a possible cancer-causing factor has come out, and it can easily cause other problems as well. Thus, you really, really do want some kind of dust collection, and quite probably you want more than a single form.

What's Out There

Dust collection today is divided into five categories. The first category is shop vacuums, then the single-stage dust collector, followed by its two-stage colleague of more effective, durable design. Cyclone dust collectors work with single- and two-stage collectors to increase the efficiency of collection. Finally, air cleaners fit up near the ceiling and use a series of filters to trap particles that escape the various other forms of dust collection in your shop.

Understanding the Features

Features differ widely as might be expected with so many different varieties. Shop vacuums use a small diameter hose — 1¼" to 2" or 2½" — and a noisy universal motor to suck up small amounts of dust and debris. You will need hose adapters for some of your machines.

Single-stage dust collectors use induction motors, which are quieter and more durable, to inhale large amounts of chips and dust. These use an upper bag to filter fine dust and a lower bag to collect the dust and other bits and pieces. With single-stage dust collectors, everything goes through the im-

peller blades, creating wear and, thus, longer-term durability problems.

Two-stage collectors use a collection drum that is placed so chips and other larger objects drop into the drum before they strike impeller blades. Again, fine dust collects in the filter bag, which need not be on top of the unit.

Cyclone collectors create an airflow that separates out the dust and chips, dropping all but the absolutely finest dust into a container at the base of the cyclone. The super fine dust goes on to collect in the bag. Again, durable induction motors are used.

Air cleaners are used to collect anything the dust collector units leave behind. The bags used on dust collectors do pass tiny particles (differing in size depending on bag weave). Air cleaner filter units pull air through a series of fine filters using a continuous-duty motor, removing anything over the designated particle size, which may be five microns or less.

Most people are familiar with traditional shop vacuums. These are basically small barrels, usually on wheels, with a motor sitting atop the barrel, a filter under the motor, extending down into the barrel, and, most of the time, a 2" diameter hose that slips into the motor head. The shop vacuum is excellent for small pick-up and even for tool attachment if you're working with a miter saw, jointer or similar small tool. It cannot begin to keep up with planers and jointers when the chips really start to fly.

These tools, especially those with smaller hose adapters, work well with circular saws, routers, sanders, miter saws and jigsaws. Similar small tools that have dust collection accessories also work nicely with shop vacuums. General shop cleanup is also easy with these tools, which do a better job of cleaning floor surfaces than all but the most sophisticated broom/dry mop on an epoxy-coated concrete floor.

Shop Vacuums

Size Needs

Choosing the right shop vacuum isn't difficult. Simply get the biggest, most powerful one you can afford. Remember, though, that dumping from one of the filled barrels into a plastic bag isn't as easy as it looks.

Power

Look for a universal motor, with a horsepower rating from 3½ to about 6½. The figures aren't true, but because almost all brands are inflated, you will see a fairly reasonable power comparison (for an explanation of this, see the chapter "What You Must Know About Motors"). The motors are all noisy, but there is noise, and then there's noise. Some create far more racket than others. Make sure the store where you buy has a liberal return policy, so you can take back a vacuum that is so loud you can't stand it. Mufflers are available to fit some brands, and they can help reduce the problem.

Capacity

The most common tank sizes start at about 12 gallons and go up to 20 gal-

Delta's model 50-665 is a two-stage dust collector allowing heavier dust particles to be trapped in the barrel, protecting the impeller.

lons. Anything more than that is unwieldy in a shop situation, though it might be handy on a plant floor or for professional cleaners.

Tank Materials

For the woodshop, there's no need to look for a material other than injection-molded plastics. The new plastics are durable, waterproof, can't rust, and are really only vulnerable to being carved on or burned.

Pricing

Shop vacuums are available priced from well under $100 to over $500. Work in the middle range, as few woodshops need a $600 shop vacuum. The extremely expensive tools are actually designed to work with drywall sanders and similar tools, and are extreme overkill for woodshops.

In Shop Vacuums, Look For:

- Overall lightness. Not all these tools have mechanically fastened hose-to-machine linkages, so towing a machine by the hose is simpler if the weight is low.
- Does it have accessories? Do accessories fit the hose easily? Do accessories fit together easily? Look for at least a crevice tool, a floor tool, a squeegee tool and rubber insert.
- How hard is changeover from wet to dry?
- Is the barrel and wheel arrangement broad-based enough for stability in movement around the shop? How large are the wheels? Larger is better.
- How noisy is it?
- How powerful is it?
- What is the barrel capacity? Check models up to 16 or 20 gallons, or down to 12, depending on your needs. Some models are smaller, designed for more dense dusts (drywall taper's sanding dust, for example).
- Does it have a handle that makes it easy to push?
- Is the switch easy to reach?
- What kind of filter does it have? The current nod goes to washable, pleated paper.

JET's model DC-1900W single-stage dust collector has a 10.6 cu. ft. capacity.

Single-Stage & Two-Stage Dust Collectors

The single-stage dust collector is the current star of the small woodworking shop. It comes in a profuse variety of sizes and power options, with two bags or four. The bags are attached to a sheet-steel central tube that accepts inlet debris and holds the impeller blades. The motor is also sometimes mounted on this large ring, though more powerful models have the motor and impeller mounted on the base. The base is a flat sheet of metal, usually with wheels. This is extremely handy for those who use a small dust collector and move it from tool to tool.

Two-stage collectors differ in appearance from single-stage — waste pieces do not drop directly into the impeller ring, but go through a bucket or other container first, dropping out the heavy stuff that wears down impeller blades quickly. The basics are essentially the same. Two-stage units tend to be more durable, yet higher priced.

Power

Induction motors drive these units. For single-stage collectors, motors range in horsepower from ½ to 5, with most of those under 2 hp either 115-volt or dual 115/230-volt. Those 2 hp and up are 230-volt single-phase. For two-stage collectors, the power range is from ¾ to 3 hp.

The ability of any dust collector to do its job is rated by cubic feet per minute (cfm). Cfm is used to determine how much power will be needed to clear dust away from any given tool. For example, most planers take from 400 to 500 cfm; jointers need about 350 cfm, as do lathes, tablesaws and smaller shapers; lathes can require up to 600 cfm; band saws need 300 cfm, as does the drill press. Router tables take about as much as shapers, though much depends on the work done.

Dust collector manufacturers have fairly precise tables for their tools. Add up your approximate needs, and, if you can, go one size larger. If you know you're never going to operate a planer, or use anything more than a table saw,

then a small unit is just fine. Select from a near multitude of ½ to 1-hp units drawing 300 or more cfm. Otherwise, add up the draw of your current tools, and give thought to possible future purchases. Even then, if your largest tool is going to be used by itself, with nothing else added, match that tool's needs and go. Give some thought to dust-collector piping runs. If you will use the collector on more than one machine, blast gates should be used to isolate each tool from the collector when not in use. When using multiple hook-ups, the piping and gates will reduce the overall available cfm performance. The longer the run from the collector to the last tool, the more power you need, in terms of cfm.

Static Pressure

Many vacuum devices are rated by static pressure readings — the higher, the better. Most are taken right at the entry to the impeller ring, and drop off, as do cfm ratings, as you add pipe or tubing. Single-stage dust collectors pull from 2.8" to 8" of water. Other models are available that pull as much as 18" of water. Though static pressure can give you a good idea of a vacuum device's ability to do its job, pay more attention to the cfm rating, as other tool manufacturers "spec" out their tools' needs in cfm rather than static pressure.

Pricing

Prices of single-stage dust collectors vary from as little as $150 to more than $5000, but those most useful in the small shop cluster in the $150 to $500 range, for the most part, which will buy you a machine that pulls from 450 to 1200 cfm.

In Single-Stage and Two-Stage Dust Collectors, Look For:

- Overall size. Is the machine going to fit in that special corner of your shop?
- Power. Is the motor going to be strong enough to do what it needs to do?
- How well do the bags filter? Many only trap particles 50 microns and

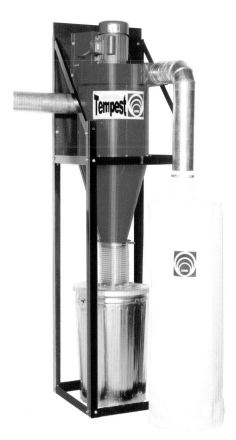

Penn State's Tempest cyclone dust collector is a 1350 cfm system, designed for professional shops.

over. Look for at least 10-micron trapping, or expect to buy more efficient bags.
- How hard are the bag clamps to remove and replace?
- How heavy is the drum or other container on a two stage?
- Is the base arrangement broad-based enough for stability in movement around the shop?
- How noisy is it? Some of the dust collectors seem to reflect their own noise out into the shop.
- Check cfm capacity as carefully as you can against your current and anticipated needs.
- What is the capacity? Some models only hold one cubic foot of waste, while others hold much more. For smaller single-stage units, two or more cubic feet is fine. Larger ones may hold 30, and that is very hard to handle for a single operator.
- Is the switch easy to reach?
- How many intake ports does it have? The range is one to six.

Cyclone Dust Collectors

Cyclonic units are available as accessories for current collectors and as complete systems. Cyclones can handle a lot of material, keep solids away from impellers and generally do a more efficient job than any other type. The cyclone is placed either in a separate location or below the impeller ring. It acts as a large piece collector, dropping those materials into a barrel below the cyclone. The impeller pulls the dust into the bag part of the system.

The JDS Air-Tech 750 air cleaner uses three filters with a 99-percent efficiency at 5 microns.

Power

Cyclone units come in 1½ hp and larger sizes (reaching 7½ hp, and even larger, in industrial models). The cheaper units may not have a motor or blower included, but may work well as an upgrade to your current single-stage system. Draw is really effective, starting at 700 cfm, and rising almost immediately to 1500 cfm. These are powerful, efficient units.

Portability

A few models are portable on a machine-to-machine basis, but most are not, though many can be fitted with waste drums that have wheels to aid dumping. Sawdust capacity is large, from 5 cubic feet on up, unless you're adapting your own system. All require 230 volts, and they are available with from one to a dozen inlet ports.

Pricing

There are affordable cyclone systems out there, though even the least expensive is much more costly than the least expensive single-stage; generally this is an industrial setup, though one that does just as well in a small shop if you can afford it. Systems start at around $300, and rise very rapidly (only about four or five are under $1000) to over $3000.

In Cyclone Dust Collectors, Look For:

- Easy assembly.
- Standard hose or duct sizes (4", 6", 8").
- How noisy is it? "Pro" shops sometimes install motors for cyclones outdoors.
- How powerful is it?
- What is the barrel capacity?
- What kind of switch does it have, or need?
- How effective are the dust bags? 50 micron? 20 micron? Smaller? Smaller is better.

Air Cleaners

Air cleaners are the air polishers in this act. They remove what's left of the lung-destroying dust from your shop air after the dust collector and vacuum finish their work. Capacities of these units are determined by the percentage of dust above a certain size that is removed, not by how much the filters collect (though the two are obviously solidly tied together). Tubular and rectangular versions are available, with mounts (depending on brand and model) for wall, ceiling and benchtop. Sizes don't vary too greatly, with rectangles of about 2' × 3' that are under a foot thick, while some of the more expensive models may be as much as 4½' long and 2' thick. Tubular styles are 8" to 10" in diameter.

THE TRANSMISSION SYSTEM: PIPE & DUCTWORK

Hoses, ductwork and pipe are all useful accessories. Depending on brand, size and other needs, you'll find blast gates in plastic and aluminum, and dust collection fittings in galvanized metal, as well as ABS plastic.

Metal ductwork is best. It is also by far the most costly, with 4" diameter straight pipe, 5' long, running upwards of $16. Elbows, blast gates, floor sweeps and Y-and-Y and T-branches cost $55 and up to $95 in galvanized steel (did I hear an 'ouch!'?), while the same parts in ABS are $4 to $8. Oh yes ... quick-fit clamps for the metal pipe are about $6 each. Figure you'll need two of those every 5'.

Flexible hose is available in 10- and 20-foot lengths. Flexible hose, though, has a corrugated, wrap-around construction that tends to trap dust, create swirls in the air flowing through and generally create problems. If you're going to use plastic (PVC) in your dust-collection system, go with 4"-diameter Schedule 40 DWV (drain-waste-vent) pipe from the local plumbing supply outfit. The price is about half what you'd pay for corrugated flex plastic, it is easier to fasten overhead, alongside and under, and is smooth inside. With the exception of blast gates, floor sweeps and some dust ports and adapters, you can get your junctions in the PVC, too. You can't glue PVC to ABS with much success, but you do not want to glue every joint of a dust collection system, anyway. If you do, you face real problems should the system ever clog. Use duct tape instead.

Remember, too, that with plastic pipe or tubing you must ground the entire system along its interior. That's nothing more than running a 14- or 16-gauge wire, unbroken, along the interior top edge of all horizontal runs and along any edge of vertical runs. Don't forget to connect that wire to ground, of course. Grounding on the dust collector motor or frame usually works well.

Efficiency

Efficiency is the way to judge filters, instead of gross power. The efficiency of these units varies widely, depending on the aim of the manufacturer. Some aim to pull lots of larger particles from the air, while others aim at pulling almost all (99 percent) of any size from the air. For the most part, the filters that pull 5-micron particles from the air have claimed efficiencies of as much as 99 percent, while those that work with smaller bits either don't state efficiency rates or work to 65 percent, or less, efficiency. Two units claim to get down to .5 micron size.

Filter Types

Three-stage filtering is available for some, with optional charcoal filters for others. Two-speed units may come with electronic or charcoal filters. Washable filters can save money.

Weights

The range is from 10 pounds to over 200 pounds. Weight generally depends on capacity.

Pricing

Small tubular models with enough air capacity to clean the air in a 10' by 15' by 8' shop as many as eight times in an hour go for around $150. Larger units, moving far more air far more rapidly,

may cost as much as $1000. There are plenty of steps in between.

In Air Cleaners, Look For:

- Overall lightness. Filter units fasten to the wall or ceiling, and the fastening is easier on both installer and the shop wall or ceiling if the unit is fairly light. It may better serve your shop to place two or more smaller units around the ceiling than one heavy, centrally mounted one.
- Do the filters replace easily?
- What is the micron range?
- What percentage of microns in that range does it remove? More is obviously better, and no 5-micron filter should do worse than 90 percent removal.
- Is the switch easy to reach?
- What kind of filter does it have? Electronic and charcoal options are available.

The Coin Flip:

Look around your shop and count up the tools that need dust collection. You may find an amazing number. Then think about how often you run more than one of those tools at a time. How often do friends come in and use your tools while you're in the shop? Size the dust collector from those figures.

Selecting the type is easier. Choose either single- or two-stage in the size

CONVERTERS AND FINE MESH BAGS

For the cost of a plastic garbage-can lid that accepts incoming and outgoing hoses (4"), you can reduce wear on a single-stage dust collector by a great deal. These $30 esparto lids fit on a standard 30-gallon galvanized or plastic trash can, and work to drop out the heavier chunks that hit the impeller blades to cause premature wear. Both bags and filters last longer, as well.

Standard dust collector bags let 5-micron material pass quite readily. Several models are available to reduce the size of particles in your shop air. For general use, 3-micron bags are a moderate cost (about $30 each), while micro-porous bags that stop everything over .3 microns are also available at a slightly higher cost ($50). When your stock bags start to show wear, replace the bags with .3 micron bags if possible.

you need. Is the brand one you can stand? If so, is the price close to right, or does a step back, up, down or sideways get you there? Worry more about capacity than about the other features, including whether or not you're dealing with a single- or two-stage or a cyclone.

Select for power, ease of assembly, ease of removal and reattachment of the lower bag and number of inlets. Obviously, then look for quality. Add in price. Remember that most single stage units can be converted at low cost to two-stage types.

For vacuums, simply select the quietest, most powerful unit you can, making sure it has a good, long cord and a decent set of accessories. Lightweight is also a big help.

For air filters, choose the one you prefer for capacity and efficiency of collected dust particles. Make sure you select a size that will give enough air changes per hour to clear your shop air — but don't expect these filters to do the job of dust collectors. Run a planer without a dust collector and even tripled air filters cannot clean the air rapidly enough.

Cyclone lids, such as this one from Veritas, can convert a simple garbage can and shop vacuum into a two-stage dust collection system.

tools | jigsaws

Why You Need One

The jigsaw — sometimes called a "saber saw" because of the shape of the blade — is the ultimate curve-cutting handsaw. It can make precise, curved cuts in any width or length of wood, plus it can tackle other materials including light steel, aluminum, plastics and surface laminates such as Formica. Most modern jigsaws pack a lot of power, with many basic models now equipped with 4-amp motors, and deluxe versions with 6-amp power plants. That's enough punch to handle 3"-thick wood easily.

Cordless jigsaws are also an option, with pretty decent performance. While you can find low-power models, most cordless designs are now packing strong 14.4- and 18-volt batteries. They will be more expensive, but if you have the need, they'll do the job.

Most jigsaws will cut at an angle, and some blades let you easily make plunge cuts — cuts that start at the interior of a piece — without drilling starter holes. Many new models have blade holders that allow for almost instant blade changes, without using a screwdriver or a wrench.

What's Out There

There are three types of jigsaws available: top-handle, barrel-grip and in-line. The top-handle design is the most common design in the U.S. because it is most like the first commercially available jigsaws. The barrel-grip is more European in its design, and while it gains converts every year, it still seems foreign to others. In use, the barrel-grip

Metabo's model STEB105 PLUS variable speed orbital jigsaw.

has a lower center of gravity to the work, reducing the tendency to "lean" the tool, but making the ultimate purchasing decision will require you to put your hands on one and make your own choice.

In-line jigsaws are new on the market and work pretty much like a home remodeler's reciprocating saw, but are much smaller. Power ranges from 3 amps on consumer models, up to 6 amps on the big boys aimed at professionals. These are fairly specialized tools and wouldn't be the recommended jigsaw purchase.

Single-speed jigsaws are still available, but why would you want one? It's much better to choose a model that offers various speed ranges which you can match to the material being cut. Variable speed makes the saw useful for more materials and more situations.

Understanding the Features

Scrolling

Scrolling is available on some jigsaws but, typically, not the professional models. Scrolling refers to the ability to turn the blade by twisting a knob on the top of the saw while you're cutting. You turn the blade, not the saw body. It's useful in some super-tight cutting situations.

Speed Adjustment

Basic speed variations are usually trigger-controlled, but there may also be a dial that lets you set a specific number of cuts per minute. This feature is useful with materials that are ruined by a too-high cutting speed — plastics that may melt, thin veneers and laminates that might chip or tear. Speed-adjusting dials also let you control cutting speed when just relying on the trigger might be difficult, such as in very tight curves. Dial location can vary widely, so find one that feels right to you.

Stroke Length

The longer (deeper) the stroke, the better the blade can clear chips, making for a cleaner, faster cut. Less costly jigsaws offer a stroke length of ⅝", while better ones have ¾" strokes. The very best models will have 1" or more stroke length.

Orbital Action

An orbital action means the blade moves slightly forward on the upstroke, and slightly back on the downstroke. This speeds up the cutting action. Not available on all jigsaws, the best allow you to adjust the orbital action from very aggressive to mild.

"Instant" Blade Changing

Changing blades is never totally automatic on any cutting tool, but jigsaws are getting close. Some models have blade change systems that literally spit the old blade out — very handy when changing blades still red hot from cutting. There are variations on that theme that require you to operate a knob, twist a lock and so on. The only way to figure out which blade change

Craftsman 3.5-amp auto-scrolling sabre saw, model 17232. The scrolling action allows you to rotate the blade without moving the tool.

system you like best is to give them a try. You might even find you prefer the old screwdriver/Allen-wrench type. One caution: Remember that blade shank types vary. Make sure your choice accepts a readily available type of blade shank. Any saw you choose should at least accept the universal bayonet-style shank.

Blade Guides

Blade guides reduce side-to-side and backward deflection of the blade. Most jigsaws have guides, but those with scrolling heads (see above) usually do not.

Base Adjustments

Base adjustment possibilities and adjuster types vary fairly widely on jigsaws. Some models, including the most expensive saws, offer no base adjustment, on the theory that what you really want is an absolutely square cut. Combined with good blade support bearings, a non-adjustable base offers easily maintained squareness. Adjustable bases do give your jigsaw more versatility, so don't rule them out. You'll find the adjustment handled by a screwdriver, Allen wrench or a lever (much preferred). Any adjustable base should have specific detents for 45 and 90 degrees, and these must be accurate and adjustable to correct any problems.

Base Covers and Anti-splinter Inserts

The jigsaw's base, the part that rides on top of whatever is being cut, can cause scratches when softer materials are being cut. That's why many "pro" model jigsaws offer replaceable plastic base inserts or covers. These covers do a wonderful job of preventing scratches on sensitive plastics and expensive wood veneers. Most saws also have replaceable anti-splinter inserts that slip into the hole in the base where the blade rides up and down. These splinter inserts work and are a worthwhile feature.

Dust Collection

Many jigsaws offer dust collection ports standard, while others make it an extra-cost option or offer no dust collection at all. We think this is a must-have feature and you should look for either a vacuum attachment or a small blower that clears sawdust from the cut line. These tools don't grind out huge amounts of sawdust, but they can quickly throw out enough fine dust to hide your cut line.

Other Good Stuff

Jigsaws multiply their usefulness when used with guides. The most common

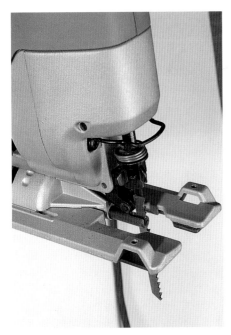

The adjustments on Porter-Cable's model 9543 uses a spring-release toolless blade-changing system.

guides are the rip fence for straight cuts, and the circle guide for cutting arcs, as well as circles. Each is fairly simple, requires a special guide holder, and tends to be brand specific, so if you need one, or expect to need one, make sure it's available before you buy the jigsaw.

There aren't many other accessories available. You may find anti-splintering devices, small inserts that fit into the base plate in order to reduce clearance around the sides and back of the blade. Or you'll find plastic base plates or base plate covers so that cuts in delicate veneers don't get scratched up by the saw's base plate. Some brands offer add-on dust collection accessories, including an attachment for the saw that then fits the hose leading to a shop vacuum.

In Corded Jigsaws, Look For:

- Find the type you prefer, barrel-grip or top-handle. Which feels right to you?
- Sturdy feel and plenty of heft to reduce the effects of vibration.
- A good fit to your hand.
- An adjustable base plate, if you need one.
- Useful speed range for your needs.
- A type of speed control (trigger-only, dial, dial-in-trigger) you find convenient.
- Easy blade changes. Allen or screwdriver in standard models; instant change in deluxe models.
- Does it accept universal shank blades?
- If it's orbital action, is it adjustable?
- What is the blade stroke? Longer tends to be better (and more expensive).
- At least a 3-amp motor.
- Is there an easily hooked-up dust collection port? (Some have none.)
- Is there a dust blower to keep the cutting line clear?
- Is there a base cover for cuts in easily scratched materials?
- Is the cutting capacity enough for your needs?

BUYING THE RIGHT BLADES

Jigsaw blades come in an almost blinding profusion of types and sizes. They're also prone to frequent breakage, bending or just plain wearing out, so never buy just one blade. Buy packages. Regardless of what you're cutting, thinner blades bend or break more often than thicker ones, so have plenty on hand before you start a job.

Basic high-speed steel blades work well for light-duty wood cutting, but for heavier work in wood and other materials, you may want to switch to bi-metal blades, which cost more but last significantly longer. Cobalt steel blades are another option, a step up from basic high-speed steel blades.

When matching a blade to the job, try to keep at least three teeth in the material at all times, although this isn't always possible with thin metals and plastics. For rough cutting, go with fewer teeth; for smoother cuts, curving cuts or when cutting metal, you want more teeth per inch. Bi-metal blades are preferred for any metal cutting. Also available are special application blades for cutting rubber, rigid foam and ceramic tile.

Should You Get A Cordless Jigsaw?

Cordless jigsaws make a lot of sense. In fact, they were one of the first cordless tools offered back at the start of the who-needs-an-outlet era. Jigsaws are, by their nature, lower-powered beasts, with motors that run from about 3 to 6 amps. A good circular saw, by comparison, needs a 10-amp motor. Thus, even the old 7.2-volt cordless jigsaws could do a decent amount of work before

Two cordless jigsaws available on the market offer varied features and ergonomics. Makita's model **4330DWA** (above) requires a screwdriver to change blades and is a top-handle design. Milwaukee's model **6267-20** (right) offers toolless blade release in a barrel-grip design.

pooping out. Today's monster 12- and 18-volt models rival anything with a cord in terms of power. As for run time, most jigsaws are only used in short spurts, so that's one more reason why going cordless makes sense.

Cordless saw features are similar to those on corded jigsaws, so you won't have to make any sacrifices there. Speeds tend to top out a bit lower at around 2800 strokes per minute, though.

The convenience of going cordless comes at a price. Cordless jigsaws cost more than corded models with similar features and, even if you have two batteries on hand, eventually you'll wear out both while the corded model just keeps humming along. Cordless tools offer supreme convenience, with no need for extensions, or even electric power, in areas where that can be a problem — and you don't need to worry about entangling or cutting through cords.

In Cordless Jigsaws, Look For:

- Adjustable orbital action.
- A long blade stroke, up to 1".
- Two batteries in the kit.
- Easy hook-up dust collection port.
- Easy-to-adjust controls for base plate angle.
- It's got to feel right in your hands, with all controls where they feel best to you.
- Is there a base cover for non-marring cuts in delicate materials?
- Is the cutting capacity enough for your needs?
- Is the cutting duration sufficient for your needs? Most good 12-volt cordless jigsaws will cut at least 35' of ¾" material before needing a fresh battery.

The Coin Flip:

Every woodworking shop needs a jigsaw, but for different reasons. While not a must-have tool, when you need to make the cuts that only a jigsaw can really handle, then it's priceless. Most of the time, though, it'll just sit on a shelf, gathering dust until called upon to perform. In football terms, jigsaws are the field-goal kickers, not the quarterbacks.

Some woodworkers we know use their jigsaws daily; others might not drag it out more than twice a year. Give some thought to your expected use. If you think you'll be cutting a lot of curves on a regular basis, then you need a top-quality corded or cordless jigsaw that will perform up to your expectations.

But if you're just messing around with curve-cutting about once a blue moon making lawn-decoration Santa cutouts (and you don't intend to do Rudolph and his buddies), then choose one of the less costly brand-name, corded jigsaws. You want a cord so you don't have to recharge a dead battery on those rare occasions you need the saw.

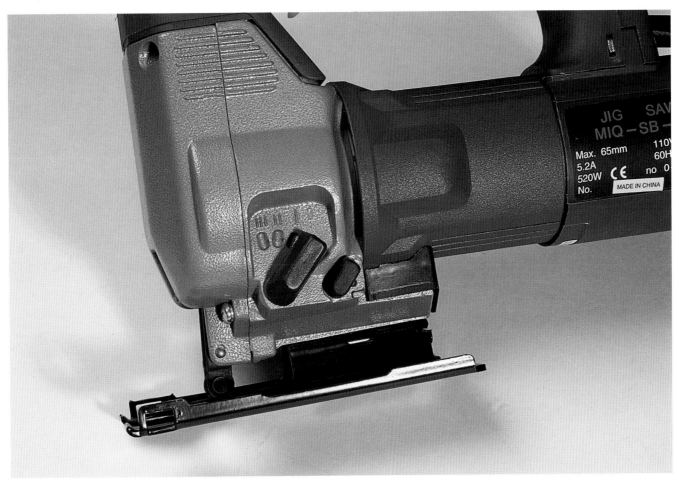

Detail of jigsaw guides and base adjustment.

Ryobi's jointer-planer, model JP155, allows space-challenged shops some of the benefits of milling machinery.

Jointers are too often viewed as being useful only for truing up two mating surfaces. While that is a major part of their use, it's only one aspect of this very helpful tool. For most power tool workshops, a jointer should be added right after the table saw, and just before the band saw. Jointers are the only power tool that safely take wind and twist out of rough stock, and are used to flatten cupped stock. In addition, a jointer lets you shape and create tapers, tenons and rabbets.

What's Out There

Jointers come in many sizes, ranging from the tiny benchtop 4" models that are under 20 pounds, up to commercial behemoths 16" wide, and so weighty and powerful they'll crack a standard concrete floor the first time they're turned on. For the smaller "pro" and amateur shops, the 6" jointer is the tool of most frequent choice, with the 8" following closely. For "pro" cabinetry, the capabilities of a 12" jointer are often necessary.

There are two basic types of jointers: benchtop and stationary. Benchtop models cost less than most stationary models, have smaller capacities and aren't as accurate. Most also lack a rabbeting ledge, and the fence may not be center-mounted (non-center-mounted fences can pivot about their mounts, creating problems). Some lighter models solve this by using two end mounts, though light-duty models often use a single-end mount.

A stationary jointer is a chunky machine, about waist high; it takes up little space. Even the biggest are not much wider than their maximum capacities (about 28" for 16" machines), and length is determined by table length. Some space for the operator in front, and some feed space, both in and out, is needed, of course, so the basic 6" jointer with a four-foot bed length may need 30" of depth, and as much as 12' of length for best use. A mobile base can simplify matters, letting you shift the jointer to the most effective place for a particular job.

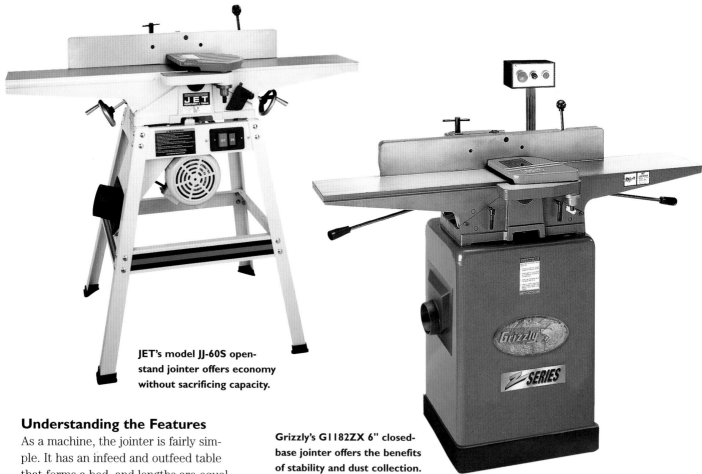

JET's model JJ-60S open-stand jointer offers economy without sacrificing capacity.

Grizzly's G1182ZX 6" closed-base jointer offers the benefits of stability and dust collection.

Understanding the Features

As a machine, the jointer is fairly simple. It has an infeed and outfeed table that forms a bed, and lengths are equal in most machines. The cutterhead fits between, and slightly below, the two tables. For stationary machines, the cutterhead is driven by a motor and belt drive mounted below the beds.

Cutterhead

The cutterhead is round, accepting two or three knives. One significant difference is that some cutterheads offer jack screws to assist in setting the knives.

Motors

Benchtop models have universal motors. Stationary jointers have induction motors. Benchtop motors range from ⅝ horsepower to 1½ hp, while 6" stationary jointers range from ¾ hp to 1½ hp. Eight-inch jointers range from 1½ hp to 2 hp, with 12" jointers ranging in the 2 to 3 hp and up range.

Fence

The jointer has a fence, varying in mounting types. The fence adjusts from very close to the operator's front edge of the jointer to just off the back of the blades, so that width of cut is infinitely variable within the capacity of the machine (4", 6", 8", 12", 16"). The fence can also be tilted, usually both toward and away from the table. Center-mount fences of good quality offer a single, secure locking point for a heavy-duty fence. Fences that mount in any other manner tend to be less secure.

Bed Length

Pay attention to the bed length. The longer the bed, the more stable your feed is going to be, which means you will get a smoother, more accurate cut. Most 6" jointers come with an overall bed length (both feed tables, plus the bridge distance over the cutters) of about 48", give or take 1" or 2". Larger (wider) jointers also have longer beds, with 66" common on 8" jointers, and around 80" fairly standard on 12" jointers. Some larger jointers have tables over 9' long.

Adjusters

Table adjusters take two forms. Lever-style adjusters have long been accepted as easier to use with heavier tables. Recently, wheel-style adjusters have become more popular and easier to adjust without overcompensating. If precision is your passion or need, then wheel adjusters are essential. If you feel jointers are not true precision machines, then levers are fine. Levers can be precise, but may take more time to get the needed exactitude.

Base

Benchtop jointers use a bench or work-table for support. Stationary jointers need an open-frame stand or enclosed base. Enclosed bases make dust collection an easier chore. Most enclosed bases come with 4" dust collection connectors. If a dust collection connector is installed on an enclosed base jointer, but the tool is not connected to a collection system, the chips and dust will

Delta's model DJ20 8" jointer offers an 8"-wide cutting capacity and an extra-long infeed table for extra support.

KNIFE-SETTING JIG

Better jointers now offer spring-loaded jack screws which provide pressure to hold the knives away from the cutterhead. For those without jack screws, a knife-setting jig is a must. Installing jointer knives isn't difficult. Pop off the blade guard, loosen the four screws (on 6" jointers) that hold each knife in place, slip out the old, slip in the new, tighten screws, put the blade guard in place and go to work. Sure. The step left out, the step where you set all three knifes to the same height as the outfeed table, is far less fun. You first set one blade to outfeed table height (or change the height of the outfeed table, should that be necessary), with the cutterhead at the 12 o'clock position. Then you carefully match the other two blades to that height. Easy. The trouble comes in maintaining knife height while tightening the screws in the knife gibs. Knife-setting jigs, available in several forms and from several companies, ease the job of holding the knives steady as you match heights across the outfeed table, and then tighten the screws. The jigs are magnet-based, with one pair clamping on the outfeed table and one on the knife. There are special models that also work with carbide blades. The steel-blade jig runs about $40. Combine that with an extra set of blades and you're always ready to go.

quickly feed back and come out around the knives as the machine operates. Open bases make dust collection harder, but do not suffer the feedback problems. Open-based machines are also usually a little cheaper.

Power
Power is usually 115- or 230-volt single-phase in machines up to 8" in capacity, and even the larger 16" machines can usually work with single-phase power. Most advertised electric motor horsepower ratings are inflated. Jointers probably suffer the least from this advertising defect. Look for at least a ¾ hp in a 6" jointer, with closed-base models offering a full horse to do the work.

Totally Enclosed Fan-cooled Motor (TEFC)
This is a very nice touch that adds to motor durability, but is slightly more costly. Non-TEFC motors do not work well with jointers because of the extremely dusty environment underneath the jointer, where the motors hang out.

Cuts Per Minute
Cuts per minute is a combination of the number of knives in the cutterhead and the rpm of the cutterhead itself — not of the motor (most motors run around 3450 rpm). The larger the number of cuts per minute, all else being equal, the smoother the resulting surface. Thus, a 3500-rpm cutterhead speed combined with four knives will give a better finish cut than will a 4000-rpm cutterhead with three knives. On a practical basis, you aren't going to notice the difference in that small a spread, but you may see different results in a two-knife 4000-rpm cutterhead and a three-knife, 4500- or 5000-rpm cutterhead.

Pricing
Benchtop jointers may be priced as low as $120, though the better ones run over $200 and as high as $550. Stationary jointers start at about $290 and rise to a mid-range of about $550 or $600 (6" closed-base models). Larger 8" jointers start at about $700 and rise to almost $2300. The foot-wide jointers kick in at around $1900 and leap to over $4600. The behemoths, the 16" jointers, begin at around $3900 and rise to over $6500.

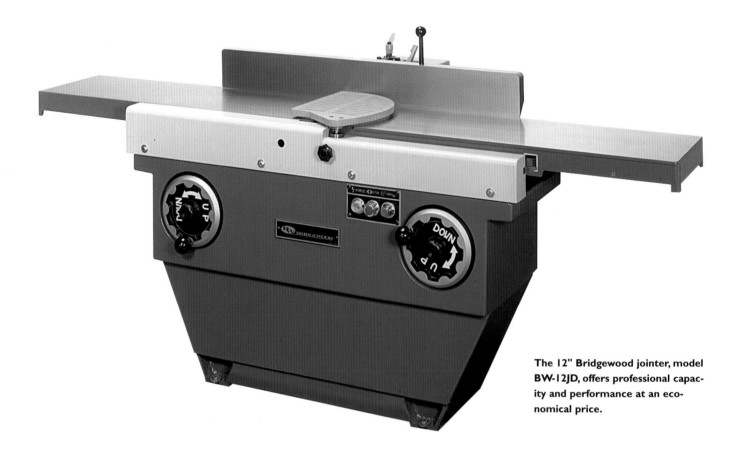

The 12" Bridgewood jointer, model BW-12JD, offers professional capacity and performance at an economical price.

MOBILE BASES

Mobile bases have become a hot accessory in the past few years. Jointers are one tool that can benefit strongly from such bases for several reasons. The mobility factor into short-term storage is foremost, because the jointer may go a week without being used. During that time, it can be rolled into a corner, or between two other tools. The space it would occupy can then used for other jobs. Also, for normal use, you may not want to move the jointer, but there may come a day when you need to feed some 8'-long boards, only to discover you have a 4' jointer table, 3' of infeed and only 2' of outfeed space. The mobile base lets you swing or roll your jointer to take advantage of any free space available. Price varies, but should be in the $45 to $70 range.

Benchtop Jointers

Benchtop machines may be ideal starter tools, or excellent for the very small shop where the tool must be placed on a bench and then, afterward, stored under the bench.

In Benchtop Jointers, Look For:

- Check the number of knives vs. rpm, to get number of cuts per minute.
- Check weight. Heavier is better even in the benchtop models.
- Horsepower.
- Availability, or lack, of rabbeting ledge.
- Is the fence center-mounted?
- Does the fence adjust easily?
- Does the fence lock securely?
- Is the fence rigid once locked?

Stationary Jointers

Stationary jointers open up the widest field for the small-shop owner. They are more versatile, faster and often easier to use. Select first for capacity, then check out the following:

In Stationary Jointers, Look For:

- Power (hp).
- 115- or 230-volt? Can it be converted if it doesn't suit your shop wiring?
- Number of knives (three is most common in 6"; some 8", 12" and 16" have four).
- Speed of cutterhead (varies from 3000 rpm to 5500 in 6" types).
- Fence type and style. Center-mounted is best.
- Does the fence adjust back and forth easily?
- Is angle adjustment of fence easily done?
- Does the fence lock securely in all planes?
- Is there a rabbeting ledge?
- What type of adjuster is used for the tables? The choice is wheel or lever, or a combination.
- What is the weight? Heavier is better, but consider floor capacities, too.
- Open stand or enclosed base? Enclosed is easier for dust collection, but causes problems when no dust collection is used.
- Ease of incorporating dust collection.
- Overall fit and finish.
- Warranty and price.

The Coin Flip:

In general, we don't recommend 4" jointers, unless you are severely strapped for space. You can buy a 6" jointer for not much more money. The most common jointer purchased is a 6" jointer, whether with an enclosed base or an open stand. If you can afford an 8", do it. You'll be happy you did later. Twelve- and 16-inch jointers are too much tool for most home woodworkers, but if you plan on working with a lot of expensive, wide lumber, then a wider jointer can be worth the money.

We strongly suggest a closed-base unit hooked to dust collection; it's less messy and more efficient.

You may want to consider the option of carbide knives rather than the standard high-speed steel knives as an upgrade.

A TOOL OF MANY USES

There are so many useful tasks for a jointer, you should never think of them merely as a way of mating together two surfaces. Among their many uses are:

Edge Jointing

To get two true and parallel edges, you first carefully joint one edge on your jointer, then rip the other on the table saw. Keep the true-jointed edge guiding along the fence. A cupped board (warped across the width) can be made flat with several passes, keeping the concave side down (if the board is no wider than the jointer's capacity). If the other side is convex, you can now use the planer to finish flattening the board, or you can, with great care to prevent the board's rocking, do the same job on the jointer. Twists and warps are treated in a similar manner, checking the results after each pass.

Shaping

For shaping operations, the jointer gives great chamfers (slicing off enough to break the edge of a corner that meets at 90 degrees). The same type of bevel can be used to form miter joints (and the degrees need not be 45 degrees each).

Creating Tapers

Tapers, such as on table legs, are easy to produce on a jointer. It is more common to taper two sides than four, but four can be done. Tapers shorter than the infeed table are readily cut in one or more passes (more is easier on the machine and gives a smoother finish). If you're tapering, for example, an 18" length, and you want a ¼" taper, set the infeed table for a ⅛" cut to start. Mark the stock at the 18" point, or set a stop block on the infeed side at 18" (this is for a stopped taper; a full-length taper does not need the stop block or mark). Place the stock with the part that is not to be tapered on the outfeed table, lowering it into position against the stop block. Feed. Repeat as often as needed (four sides, four feeds; two sides, two feeds). Now, reset the depth at ¼" and repeat the process.

Rabbeting

Rabbeting ledges on jointers are useful for making this common joint. The ledge is nothing more than a widening of the infeed table, with a dropped section of the outfeed table following. Because the cutter guard must be removed for this operation, many people consider it unsafe, and it can be. Use exceptional care to keep your hands on the feed blocks and away from cutters. Remove the guard. Bring the fence in to the distance from the table/cutter edge that equals the rabbet depth. Lower the infeed table about half the depth of the rabbet (it is always safer, and gives a smoother finish, to do rabbets in two cuts). Make the first pass on all pieces. Lower the table to the final depth and make the last passes on all pieces. Replace the blade guard immediately when done. (Note: OSHA regulations do not allow this rabbeting procedure in professional shops.)

tools | lathes

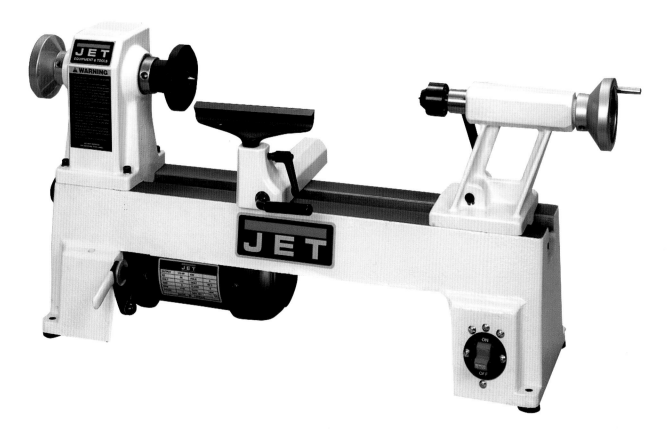

When you get right down to it, lathes are great fun. There's something very satisfying about reducing a spinning chunk of raw wood into something useful or pretty. Lathes offer an easy-start, slow-finish style of woodworking. It often seems more like art than woodworking. Lathes require very little training and practice to get started, so even freeform shapes are simple and easy. Of course, to be really good on the lathe — to be in full control of your creativity — training and lots of practice are required.

From a wholly practical perspective, lathes help you make any rounded object, from a pen barrel to bowls to spindle legs for furniture. Fluting (decorative grooves the length or leg of a column) can also be done on a lathe, and even thread cutting.

JET's model JML-1014 benchtop lathe is designed for small turnings such as pens, bowls and candlestick holders.

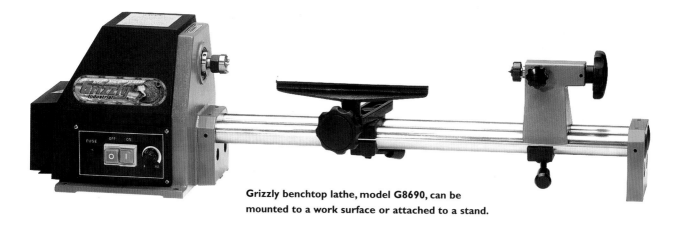

Grizzly benchtop lathe, model G8690, can be mounted to a work surface or attached to a stand.

What's Out There

There are four lathe types available: mini-lathes, benchtops, floor models and specialized bowl-turning lathes.

Mini-lathes fit on your workbench or come with a small stand. They're actually an evolution of earlier benchtop lathes, but smaller. These mini-lathes are used for turning small items, such as pens.

Benchtop lathes also are designed to be bolted to a workbench surface (you supply one or you can purchase optional stands) and come close to the abilities and capacities of floor models.

Stationary floor model lathes are the big boys of this bunch, designed to turn out massive projects as long as 50" and as large as 20" in diameter.

Bowl lathes are odd-looking ducks that lack a tailstock. As you can figure out, their purpose in life is to turn bowls. Most will create bowls from 2' to 4' in diameter, but you can find models that will carve out incredible 20' bowls if that's what you really need. These are very specialized tools and, as such, little space will be dedicated to them here.

Understanding the Features
Bed

A lathe starts with a bed made of cast iron or steel tubing, with cast iron usually considered the better choice because the more solid the bed, the more accurate the lathe will be. As with most woodworking tools, heavy is better because the weight absorbs vibration. The bed must be accurately machined, correctly assembled and have great strength.

Headstock

The headstock (located on the motor) has a pencil-point center with four chisel-like knives that push into the turning material to hold it while it turns. Lathe speed is controlled here by a series of pulleys and belts (you move the belt to different pulleys to alter the speed) or a variable speed motor that you set with a dial. Lathe speeds typically range from 500 to 3000 rpm. Some lathes offer headstocks that swivel 90 and 180 degrees to allow you to turn larger pieces by working away from the bed. This is called "outboard" turning.

Tailstock

At the right end of the lathe is the tailstock. You move the tailstock to accept different length material between the centers. Mounted on the tailstock is the "live center," which is a pencil-type point fitted to a free-spinning bearing.

Tool Rest

Between the tailstock and the headstock is the tool rest. Tool rests come in various shapes (straight, long, short and S) to match specific tasks. It's where the tool rests as it shaves away material. Adjustable for height and distance from the work, it's got to lock solidly in place on the tool bed, yet adjust easily.

Benchtop and Mini-Lathes

Mini-lathes are the offspring of benchtop models. They'll easily fit on your workbench and are intended for turning pens, knife handles and other lightweight projects. As long as you don't

get ambitious and start asking these little Shetland ponies to be wood-hogging workhorses, you'll probably be quite satisfied with the results. Generally mini-lathes offer capacities from 5" over the bed and 12" between centers, to about 10" × 18" between centers.

Benchtop lathes may offer up to 5" turning diameters and 38" between centers, only a bit behind full-size floor models in capacity. These lathes typically weigh under 200 lbs., compared to 250 or more for stationary models. Of course, a lot of that weight difference comes from the lack of a stand, which you supply.

Power

Rated power on lathes jumps all over the lot, as do speed ranges. The actual and rated power may differ widely but, for most work, starting at 1/2 hp is fine. Mini-lathes are lighter, smaller, designed to work with smaller stock, and may present as little as ⅛ horsepower, with sufficient power to do all the tool's designated work. Benchtop models then rise to about a 1 hp rating. Prices do not grow according to the power ratings, but do change according to drive type, whether or not the head has a spindle for bowl turning at one end — or is reversible for bowel turning — and overall quality. You can pick up a standard-size benchtop lathe for as little as $180, or spend nearly $2000. (Two of the models in this range offer swiveling headstocks, with 30" bowl capacities). If bowl turning interests you, check to see that the lathe offers outboard turning.

Power Transfer

Power transfer is a feature that can be troublesome, because some types force you to change belts on step pulleys (SPD) every time you change speeds. This isn't a critical factor, and was the only way to go on small lathes for a great many years. It does, though, force an extra action and take time. Today, numerous benchtop lathes offer electronic drive (ED) that changes speeds with the turn of a knob. The Reeves drive (RD) is another animal, and is fairly complex. It is found in the most costly lathes, and is a shifting cone-belt arrangement that works with a shaft handle that the turner moves to change speeds.

Speeds

Speed ranges determine how well you can do most kinds of work. The lower speeds are great for roughing out stock. The higher speeds allow fast cutting and finishing. And the speed ranges are not like drill speed ranges, within a few rpm of each other. These hop around a lot. One lathe has a lower speed of 24 and a top speed of 4000 (both very low and fairly high). Another may offer 5 to 3000, exceptionally low (beaten only by the machine that turns 0-2750) and moderately high. The average lathe, whether ED or SPD or RD, tends to run in the 400 to 2700 range, which is a better-than-decent range for most turning.

Pricing

Pricing may jump from under $200 to almost $2000, but there is a clustering in mid-range, with top lathes going for $400 to about $1000. Good beginner lathes kick in around $300 and rise to about $600. Lathes for experts kick in at $700 or so and ride up to the top.

In Benchtop and Mini-Lathes, Look For:

- Size. What size turnings do you plan to do? Choose the size lathe that fits your projects. Pen turnings, small balls, goblets — all fit superlatively with mini-lathes. For larger work, including most spindles, look for a lathe that has at least a 30"-length capacity.
- There must be plenty of material in the lathe. The more it weighs, the more stable it is. Some turners weigh down the benches or frames of their lathes with sandbags for extra vibration dampening.
- Does the tailstock move easily once unlocked? Are the locks easy to tighten? Does the lock hold solidly?
- Does the tool rest move easily once it is unlocked? This applies to both horizontal and vertical locks. Does the tool rest's lock hold solidly? This is an imperative.
- How good is the fit and finish? You'll pay for a better fit and finish, but it may be worth it.
- Are the ways cast iron or steel tubing? Machined cast iron allows easy movement, and the most secure locking.
- Is there enough power for your anticipated turning needs?
- What kind of speed control is there? Electronic is easiest to use on moderate-cost lathes. Step pulleys are more common right now. An RD comes on only one brand of benchtop lathe.
- What kind of removal is used for the tapered live center? Some use a rod driven into the headstock to pop the center out, while the better machines use a dual nut that drives the device out more easily.
- Is there an indexing feature on the head? This is only important if you think you'll do some fluting at some time, though it may also ease drawing some layout lines.
- Does it have outboard turning capacity?
- What is the weight? A weighty machine is better, within reason.

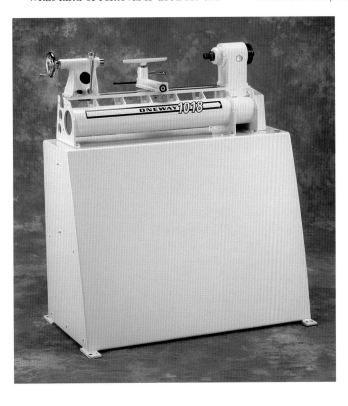

A mini-lathe from Oneway, model 1018, is designed for serious hobbyists or professional turners.

SPECIAL CHUCKS

Chucks work to hold odd-shaped and sized materials, or oversized materials, without doing extreme damage to the material. There are literally dozens of different jaw set-ups that fit the chucks to traditional and special faceplates so that the turner can concentrate on the work, instead of worrying about whether or not it will stay secured, or get ruined. Prices on chucks range from about $180 to over $280. Beyond the chuck, special jaws are needed, and those run from $35 up to more than $140.

Floor-Model Lathes

The floor-model lathe is the big brother of the bigger benchtop lathes. The smallest floor-model lathes have capacities of 12" diameter by 35" or 36" or 37" in length, while the bigger ones turn up to 24" by 50". The work done is the same, but you can do more of it, more quickly, than with lighter-duty tools. Prices also tend to be higher. The cheapest stationary lathe is going to run a little over $325 delivered, while the most costly slips past $4500.

Speed and Drives

Speed ranges don't differ a whole lot from benchtops, with a low of zero and a high of 3500 rpm. For the most part, the low is a little lower, with more machines capable of slowing down to under 300 rpm, but the high is about the same. Control types are the same, with step pulleys dominating, and Reeves drives present from three or four manufacturers. Electronic drives are appearing, even in the high price ranges, but in the lower price ranges, you get either Reeves or step pulleys for drives in this category.

Power

Here there's a mild step up, with ½ hp about as low as things get. Most are in the ¾ and 1 hp category, until you hit the high-end stuff where 1½ hp to 2 hp dominates. Weight is highly variable here, too, with lightweight stationary lathes under 150 pounds, but most are in the 250 plus pound area, rising to a high of 850 pounds. As always, with stationary tools that exceed 250 pounds in weight, give careful thought to location and to getting the tool to that location from the back of the semi doing the delivery.

Bed Materials

Beds come in the same selection of materials you find in benchtop lathes, now with the addition of wood. Wood is used in two custom lathes where bed length is up to the customer. It is in the

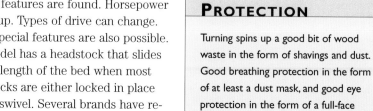

Delta floor-model lathe, model 46701, comes complete with stand and a pivoting headstock for outboard turning.

stationary lathe category that many custom features are found. Horsepower can go up. Types of drive can change. Other special features are also possible. One model has a headstock that slides the full length of the bed when most headstocks are either locked in place or only swivel. Several brands have reversible motors (said to be good for sanding some projects), while another offers an optional reverse. At least one lathe can be completely built to customer specifications.

Pricing

As with benchtop lathes, prices tend to cluster (though here only a little bit), with full capacity models running from $450 to $2500. That's still a pretty wide swing, and the major part of the cluster is near the upper end. For beginners, with two or three exceptions, benchtop lathes are a better way to go.

PROTECTION

Turning spins up a good bit of wood waste in the form of shavings and dust. Good breathing protection in the form of at least a dust mask, and good eye protection in the form of a full-face shield are indisputable needs. For the more active forms of turning — large spindles and heavy fluting done with a router and jig, for example, more active lung protection in the form of a respirator is needed. One-piece respirators and face shields are available.

For those using a face shield and having problems with fogging inside, there's an old motorcyclist's trick that works: Just under your nose (mark with a crayon while wearing the shield), drill a diamond of ¼" holes spreading about 2½" to 3" wide. This helps even with a dust mask on, though not as much as when the nose is free.

3 TURNING TOOLS

A good set of turning tools will have from five to eight pieces. Avoid the cheapest of the cheap. If you're just beginning, you'll probably want to avoid the top of the line stuff, too, because a single tool can cost more than a cheap set. Look for a good mid-range set with a small selection of skews, gouges and parting tools. Get used to those, and then, one tool at a time, move up to the top-of-the-line tools. Somewhere in there, you'll probably want to buy a set of miniature turning tools for the fine detail work. Costs can range from about $85 a set on up past $300 for the full-sized tools, and from $50 to $100 a set for the miniature tools. Add a set of top grade calipers, inside and out, along with a divider, in at least 8" size. A 4" set also is a help when making small turnings. Cost ranges from $20 to $50.

In Floor-Model Lathes, Look For:

- Size. What size turnings do you envision? Stationary lathes are even great with small turnings because the extra weight aids stability, which makes for very smooth turning. If you anticipate a lot of small turning, with a moderate amount of large turning, you might consider a stationary lathe.
- There must be plenty of material in the lathe beds. Beds must be solid enough not to twist, regardless of the material from which they are manufactured.
- Does the tailstock move easily?
- Are the tailstock locks easy to tighten?
- Does the tailstock spin the center in easily?
- Do the tailstock locks hold solidly?
- Does the tool rest move easily once it is unlocked? This applies to both horizontal and vertical locks.
- Is the tool rest easy to remove?
- Does the tool rest's lock hold solidly? The only movement at the tool rest should be the turner moving the tool.
- How good is the fit and finish? You can save some money here if rough castings don't interfere with the action of the machine.
- Are the ways cast iron or steel tubing? Machined cast iron allows easy movement, and the most secure locking. Tubes allow the easiest positioning and slickest movement of the tailstock.
- Is there enough power for your anticipated turning needs? Most turning work can be easily done with a 0.5-hp motor.
- What kind of speed control is there? ED is not found on lower-cost stationary lathes. Step pulleys are available, but Reeves drives seems to dominate. It works well and is time-proven.
- Is there an indexing feature on the head? This is important if you think you'll do some fluting.
- Does it have outboard turning capacity? Most, but not all, stationary lathes offer outboard turning or treat it as an option.
- What is the weight? Weight makes the lathe more stable, but harder to ship, move around and set up.

The Coin Flip:

The créme de la créme of spindle lathes is found in the big production models or the customized brands. Yet the average person has no need of that kind of power, no place to put the lathe, and might have to mortgage at least the garage to pay for the tool. The first step is to decide on the size and type of turning you wish to do. Then look for lathes that will help you carry out your wishes.

If you want to make pens, shaving brushes, yo-yos or any of a host of other small items as artistic or market challenges, then give careful thought to a mini-lathe. These are not cheap lathes, with prices ranging from $150 to over $1350, but there is a good mid-range cluster between $200 and $300 that offers superb value. Usually, small projects are more easily done on small lathes.

For spindle projects over 12" or 18" long, benchtop lathes work well for many people, allowing the turning of all sorts of furniture parts, including cannonball bedposts, table legs and similar parts. These lathes also offer the capacity to do small turnings such as pens, while expanding the creative craft horizon.

Stepping up, or over, to stationary lathes may mean an increase in cost and weight, but can also offer a more solid base for turning. The cost doesn't have to rise (the top-priced benchtop lathe is almost $2000, while the lowest cost stationary lathe is around $300), but the quality tends to keep track of cost, at least to a point. The primary advantage here is the possibility of increased power, and a stable base for the lathe with no need to depend on a stand you buy or a bench you make. Much of a turner's success depends on the weight and stability of the base under the lathe.

Moving to a bowl lathe is more of a career decision than any of the other choices. Until a turner has a reasonable amount of experience, buying a moderately expensive single-use lathe is not a superb way to use cashed-in E-bonds.

The world of miter saws has grown immensely in the past decade. Not too long ago, there was only the conventional miter saw, a pivoting head tool with a rotating table that could be set to cut 45-degree right and left angles, and any in between. A few models even went beyond 45 degrees. There were 8¼" models and 10" models, and that was about it. For those of us who needed to cut more angles in different planes, handsaws were still the only way to go. Then the compound miter saw descended, and we could do the work. Not long after that, the sliding compound miter saw arrived.

A miter saw makes it far easier to square ends of boards, or cut specific angles. For most shops, the miter saw replaces attempts to crosscut small stock and to make miters on a table saw. The table saw is something of a losing proposition for that kind of work, unless special jigs are made. A radial arm saw can do the work a miter saw does, but at two expenses: space, money and, usually, less precision.

What's Out There

Miter saws come in various configurations: conventional, compound and sliding compound. Each has its unique points — prices vary as features increase.

Understanding the Features
Fences
The fence for the conventional miter saw has to accept a blade and head coming in at an extreme angle from only a single direction, so it does not have a very large gap. Fences exist in two parts. Where the gap doesn't support the work pieces you intend to cut, you can install an auxiliary fence that covers more of the distance. This is more easily done with a conventional miter saw than with a compound, which must have the fence cut at an angle from the left and, sometimes, from the right, as well.

Get An Angle On It
All miter saws will cut angles to both the right and left, with maximum angles of 45 degrees right, 45 degrees left at the low end, and a maximum angle of 60 degrees left and 50 degrees right on one machine ... 51 degrees left, 59 degrees right on another. The few extra degrees added is great for working on molding that has to fit projects that are not perfectly square. You can make very thin trimming cuts on a miter saw, but you can "creep-trim" until you get the angle right only on those with extra degrees of miter. Of course, it you lop off far too much the first time, you must start over with a new piece, since changing angles shortens the work in a hurry.

Materials
Castings may be iron or aluminum. This becomes obvious in weight, which runs from a low of about 19 pounds to a high of about 55 pounds. Weight is important as a stabilizing factor when the tool is in use, though it makes sense to

Black & Decker miter saw, model 1720.

nail, screw or clamp any of these tools to a workbench. It is also a factor in mobility. It is easier to toss a 25- or 30-pound tool in the back seat of a car, or in the back of a pick-up, than one that weighs 50 pounds or more.

Handles
Three handle types are generally available, all with the switch lying under the trigger finger. The D-handle may be vertical or horizontal and, in one or the other position, is the most popular. It is easy to use and gives a secure grip. There is also a slightly curved banana-shaped handle on some machines. These are also comfortable and have the trigger located under the finger. Check to see which suits you best.

Conventional Miter Saws

Standard, or conventional, miter saws are available in abundance from a variety of makers. Blade sizes today start at 8¼" for modestly priced models, and run up to 15". The 10" miter saw is fairly basic, while the 12" model is for those with bigger things to cut. Capacities range from a low of 2⅛" × 4⅞" (thickness and width) to a high of 4¾" × 7⅞" on the monster 15" model. Dust collection is by bag or vacuum port, with most models having both.

Safety

These machines sling small off-cuts at a ferocious speed, almost always to the cut-off side of the blade. (If you're cutting right, then that small piece is on the right — if it catches a tooth the wrong way, you suddenly feel like a participant in an old western movie, as you are surrounded by ricocheting noises.) The guards are generally decent, if not great, and some saws have blade brakes. The brakes serve more as a quick-stop that lets you move on to the next cut, rather than as a true safety feature. The preferred safety technique is to lower the blade into the cut, hold it there until it comes to a stop and then raise it. Letting the blade lift out of the cut while it maintains spin is only going to sling bits and pieces around the shop.

Ryobi's 10" Super Miter Saw, model TS254.

Prices

You have your own acceptable price range. Low-end conventional miter saws may cost under $120. Top-of-the-line (size and quality) conventional miter saws run up to almost $660 for a big 15" saw, though most are under $200.

In Conventional Miter Saws, Look For:

- Size. 8¼" models are suitable for minimal thickness and width, 10" for greater, 12" is the most practical for woodworkers (the single 15" is too pricey for most of us).
- Is there a sturdy feel, plenty of beef

in the overall construction to reduce the effects of vibration?
- Does the handle feel good?
- Generally good fit and finish.
- Is it aluminum or cast iron? Weight is the primary concern here; it tends to be good for stability, bad for portability. Define your needs.
- Useful power for your needs. Smaller blade diameters need less power. The range is 9 amperes to 15 amperes, with most at 15, then 13.
- Easy-to-hook-up dust collection port (most have an easily removable bag on the port).
- Does the blade guard retract easily and positively? If it doesn't do so

now, it will later as the machine builds up sawdust in its parts.
- Is there a blade brake? If not, expect to wait longer between cuts.
- Is there a depth control? Is it easy to set?
- How many positive stops right and left does the tool offer? More is better. There may be as many as nine.
- Check adjustability or replacement of throat plate.
- Are the location of controls user-friendly?
- Are hold-downs provided? Are they easy to use?
- Are tools to make adjustments stored on the saw?

Compound Miter Saws

With the advent of the compound miter saw, more complex cuts became available, without a need to go back to the radial arm saw or the table saw. Compound and bevel cuts are now made in a single pass on a single light-weight machine. Like the miter saw, the compound miter saw (CMS) has a swiveling base into which the blade fits when cutting miters. It also has a pivoting head in the horizontal plane to allow bevel cuts at angles of as much as 48 degrees. A few will even swing the other way a degree or two. The CMS functions differently from the basic miter saw when used to cut bevels. With a pivoting head, a slightly larger gap in the fence and an angle sliced off the left part of the fence, there isn't an immense of amount of difference.

Weight and Price

A CMS weighs more than a conventional miter saw. Extra bearings (with slightly larger castings to hold those bearings) and extra controls each add a few ounces to the weight. The machine, working two planes, demands more precise tolerances all around and prices tend to show this, with the lowest priced CMS about $180. Prices rise over $300 for 12" versions, and there's one dual bevel 10" CMS out there that is priced under $300. Most compound miter saws are 10" and weigh from about 39 to 58 pounds.

Capacities

Cut capacities seem to require an extra dimension these days. But with the added dimension, capacity is reduced. Capacities range from a low of 2½" × 5⅝" to a high of 2½" × 7⅛".

Power

Power ranges change slightly, with only a single 9-ampere model currently out there for the only 8¼" CMS. All the rest are 13- and 15-ampere models. The more complex, often thicker, cuts made with a CMS demand the extra power.

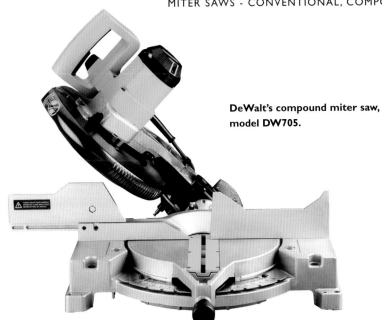

DeWalt's compound miter saw, model DW705.

Blade Changes

When you're at the store, check to see how easily a blade can be removed and replaced. This is more of a struggle on some machines than others; try to make sure it's not a struggle on yours. On a typical CMS, a flap is loosened and raised to expose the arbor bolt. The spindle lock holds the blade, while you wind out the bolt and remove the washer. Remove the blade at this point to find out if the clearances have been designed too tight. If the blade slips easily into your hand, fine. If not, you have to wiggle it around to get it out. Unless you want such a fight every time you change a blade (admittedly, with carbide-tipped blades, that may only be every year or so in the average shop), pass on that machine. And, of course, put the demonstrator blade back on, tighten the arbor bolt and replace the cover. It's not nice to make a grown salesperson cry. This possible problem extends to a few models in the slide compound category, as well.

In Compound Miter Saws, Look For:

- Size. 10" is basically the most sensible minimum for a CMS, 12" is practical for most woodworkers.
- Is the overall construction sturdy enough to reduce the effects of vibration?
- Does the handle feel good, regardless of design?
- Is there a good fit and finish? Top-name brands all have good fit and finish. Tools such as this are not low enough in price anywhere to accept a poor fit and finish.
- Is it aluminum or cast-iron? Weight is the primary concern here; it tends to be good for stability, bad for portability. Define your needs.
- Is there enough power for your work? Blades with smaller diameters need less power. Again, the range is 9 amperes to 15 amperes, with most at 15, then 13.
- Is there an easy-to-hook-up dust collection port (most have an easily removable bag on the port)?
- Does the blade guard retract easily and positively? If it doesn't do so now, it will later as the machine builds up sawdust in its parts.
- Is there a blade brake? If not, expect to wait longer between cuts.
- Is there a depth control? Is it easy to set?
- How many positive stops right and left does the tool offer? More is better.
- Is the switch easy to use?
- Check adjustability or replacement of throat plate.
- Are the location of controls user-friendly?
- Are hold-downs provided? Are they easy to use?
- Are tools to make adjustments stored on the saw?

Sliding Compound Miter Saws

You love 'em or you hate 'em. Sliding compound miter saws are the top of the line, with the greatest crosscut capacities, and are available in both single compound and dual compound models. Prices rise quickly for this type of miter saw. The lowest is priced at about $100 more expensive than a moderately priced CMS. Blade sizes start at 8½" and rise to 12". Prices start in the low $200 and rise to over $600. Features increase as the prices rise.

Porter-Cable's 10" sliding compound miter saw, model 3807.

Slides

The big bear in these woods is actually a slide tube — and the bearings on which the head rides on the tube. For the most part, slide compound miter saws (SCMS) use two slides (tubes of polished steel) and a single set of bearings located wherever the manufacturer determines is best for the tube vs. head stability. Three tubes have been used by some manufacturers. There is some disagreement as to what is the best configuration of the tubes: Vertical positioning is popular, but some of the best saws use two tubes positioned horizontally. One or two saws use a single, larger tube and more bearings or larger bearings. For basic woodshop use, almost any well-made SCMS should work well and last a long time.

The best spot-check is usually a cut or two at extreme angles to check accuracy. Make sure any tool you buy is readily returnable. That is even more important with tools that are in this higher price range.

Power and Capacities

As with other miter saws, SCMS versions have different blade sizes, with power ranging from a low of 9.5 amperes to a high of 15 (although there is also a single 18-volt cordless SCMS now available). The bigger the blade's diameter, the more power required to drive it through maximum-capacity cuts. And it is the capacity that is startling — as SCMSs all top their country cousins by

BLADES

Blades are all-important to miter-saw efficiency. Using a 24-tooth blade in an 8½" miter saw is great for rough stock. Using the same blade to cut finish miters for picture or furniture frames is a horror. Using a 60-tooth finish cut blade for cutting rough lumber is OK on a very occasional basis. Doing this often is a bad thing. It takes longer to make the cut, draws more power from the saw more often and is rough on the fancy (expensive) blade.

Select blades for specific uses and change them when uses change. For 8½" miter saws, use cut-off blades with 60 teeth for shop work and specific rough cut and 24- or 30-tooth blades for construction-type work. For 10" diameter miter saws, select a 60- or 80-tooth blade for smooth cuts. For general rough work, use a 40-tooth blade. For 12" diameter saws, you can use an 80- or 96-tooth blade for glass smooth cuts and a 60-tooth blade for rougher work.

Unless you are consistently having problems with power (the blade jams in the cut, for example), do not use a thin kerf blade in a miter saw. There is too much tendency to wander.

Always keep blades sharp. An old adage states that sharpening a blade before it really needs it saves money. The reasons are simple. You don't waste material with bad cuts. Your sharpener doesn't have to take off as much material to get the blade back to great cutting shape.

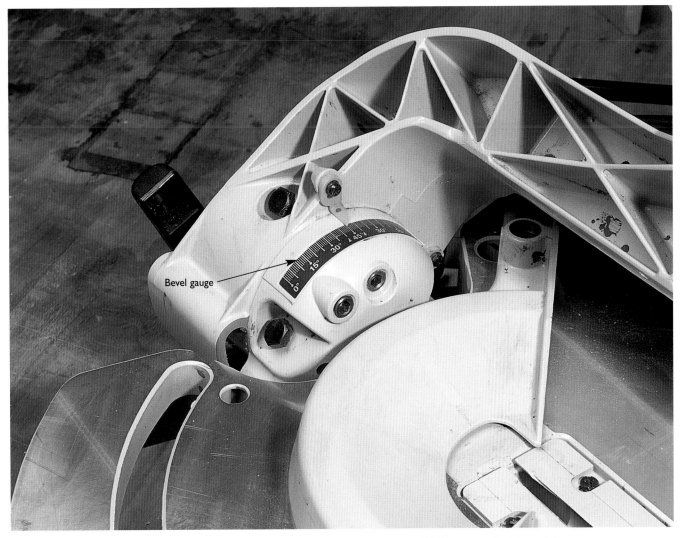

Bevel gauge

The Makita LS1013 is a dual compound sliding miter saw, allowing the blade to bevel 45 degrees to the left or right.

a considerable amount. Even the little 8½"-blade tools can slice their way through 2⅝"-thick lumber a full foot wide (at 90 degrees). Larger blades — 12" — can reduce lumber of 3¹¹⁄₁₆" thickness and 12⅜" width to parts. Actual maximum cut depth is greater on another brand, that gives a 4½" depth and 12" width. Angles cut may vary from a top of 60 degrees to 60 degrees (right and left) to 45 and 45. Bevel angles range from 45 degrees to zero on standard single-bevel models to as much as 48 degrees right and 48 degrees left on dual SCMS tools. As you might guess, prices rise in accordance with these increases in capacity.

Short of rolling out a radial arm saw (most 10" radial arm saws have a crosscut capacity of about 15"), the SCMS does the job. If you really need greater width, then one of the super-capacity radial arm saws may be needed (some 14" models offer a 29" crosscut).

Safety and Convenience

These saws are not as easily transported as their more compact brethren. The long tubes extend past the rear, they weigh more. (Low weight is about 37 pounds and the average is much higher. The high is about 57 pounds.) More aluminum is used in construction in an effort to keep the weight rational. Check blade guards for ease of operation. Check the handle for feel, and trigger for operation and feel. See if the tool has a carrying handle and a simple, fast lock for the head. The table must be locked to carry these tools more than 18" or so, which is no problem. Head locks can pose a problem, but

most are fairly sensible.

Dust collection is almost identical to that of the conventional miter saws and non-slide compound miter saws. A dust port extends from the back casting of the saw or from the top blade guard. That port takes a bag or may be hooked up to a collector or vacuum, with the appropriate adapters.

Fences

Fences are similar to those on non-slide compound miter saws, which means the inside end on the left is clipped off for the SCMS, and both sides are clipped off on the dual slide compound miter saw.

Fences are adjustable and, as with all these saws, it may pay to mount an auxiliary fence that closes the blade gap. If you do add such a fence, make sure that the angle of the fence matches the angle of the stock fence, or the blade will hit it.

In Sliding Compound Miter Saws, Look For:

- Size. For a SCMS, an 8½" model works well for many woodworkers. Getting the use out of a 10" or 12" SCMS is difficult in a small, non-commercial shop, and the dual SCMS is an even bigger expense to justify.
- Is the overall construction sturdy enough to reduce the effects of vibration? With the long slides stuck out the back, the head and pivots must be exceptionally sturdy.
- Does the handle feel good, regardless of design?
- Is the handle easy to operate, and the switch easy to use?
- Is there a good fit and finish? You must have a good fit and finish to show internal quality. If the finish is poor, look elsewhere, regardless of price. These are complex tools and can be easily knocked out of whack; if they aren't well-made at the factory, they may be out of whack the moment you buy it.
- What's the weight? Weight is good for stability, bad for portability. Define your needs.
- Is there enough power for your work? Blades with smaller diameters need less power. Again, the range is 9.5 amperes to 15 amperes, with most at 15, then 13, and a few at 10.
- Is there an easy-to-hook-up dust collection port?
- Does the blade guard retract easily and positively? If it doesn't do so now, it will later as the machine builds up sawdust in its parts.
- Is there a blade brake? If not, expect to wait longer between cuts.
- Is there a depth control? Is it easy to set?
- How many positive stops right and left does the tool offer? More is better.

- Check adjustability or replacement of throat plate.
- Are the location of controls user-friendly?
- Are hold-downs provided? Are they easy to use?
- Are tools to make adjustments stored on the tool?

The Coin Flip:

If you need a minor number of fairly narrow crosscuts to square up stock under 6" wide and less than 3" thick, give serious thought to one of the standard miter saws, with a 10" blade. For larger stock with fairly simple angle-cutting needs, think about a similar saw that has a 12"-diameter blade. You should be able to outfit your shop for well under $200 or, at most, $250. For more complex angle cuts, start looking for the 10"-diameter compound miter saws in various models. You can select from a starting price of around $175 and rise rapidly, but even the 10" dual compound model comes in under $220. The bigger saws, as always, cost more. Going for a 12" CMS will cost you over $300.

If you need to get really fancy and have lots of large material, width or thickness or both, then the SCMS becomes the tool of choice. For not-so-thick, but still fairly wide, use consider

A 12" sliding compound miter saw, such as DeWalt's DW708, offers the largest cross-cut capacity of any miter saw type.

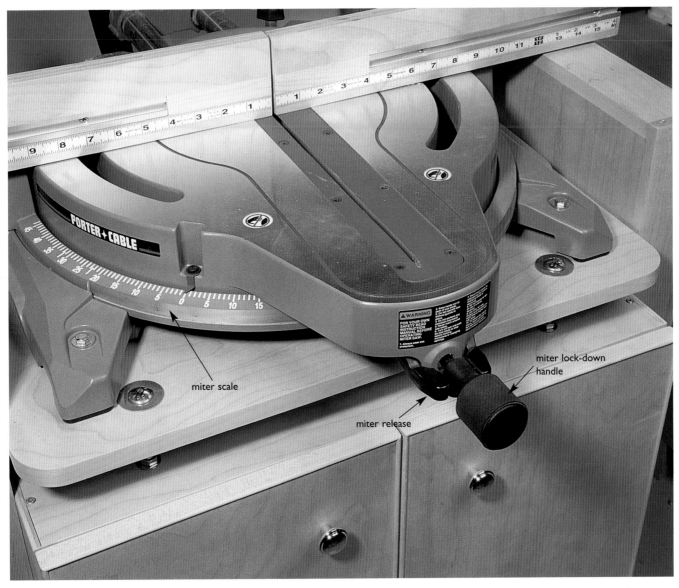

Most miter saws have set stops at common miter settings, but can be locked in place between settings using the lock-down handle.

the several 8½"-diameter slide compound miter saws out there. These do an excellent job for most woodworking purposes, and one is available as a dual SCMS. Prices start at under $275 for the small saws. For larger capacities, prices rise quickly and proportionately. As with most tools, you must identify your actual needs and plans before making the coin toss. If you need to miter 3"-thick by 8"-wide boards consistently, then buying a 10" standard miter saw is a waste of money. If you need to cut 4"-wide boards square most of the time, then buying a $650 dual SCMS is a bigger waste of money.

WORKSTATIONS

Miter saws almost demand their own workstations — if not immediately, then soon after purchase. There are a wide number of commercially available workstations that are easy to use and set up. The workstation should have an adjustable rail/stand upon which the miter saw can mount and be stable and totally steady. The stand must be heavy enough and wide-based enough to provide support for slide compound miter saws, if that is what you use. Drop one of those saws backward onto its slides from 3' up, and you face major repairs. Extensions to each end are needed, with practical limits at

about 3' or so. Extensions should have easily adjustable (for height) work supports.

Some workstations offer a back rail that has a rule on it and an adjustable stop. These are helpful, but add to the cost.

Shop-built workstations are also excellent and often far better than the commercial units, at least for the woodworker. The commercial units are primarily designed for contractors, with portability a big feature. Any bench design can be adapted with supports built in at each end to hold stock to be cut, and stock that has been cut.

The planer does two jobs, but it does them very well if you get a good one. It is the tool of choice for smoothing parallel surfaces of rough-cut boards. It also is the tool of choice for thicknessing boards so that they are the exact thickness needed for a particular project. This makes it ideal for woodworkers who wish to buy rough lumber to save money or to gain more control over their materials.

What's Out There

Not too long ago, the standard shop planer was a huge and incredibly costly tool. About 15 years ago, Ryobi introduced the first portable planer (the AP10), and revolutionized small-shop woodworking with a relatively low-cost tool that was easy to move around and that could be stored easily when not in use. Today, we have two primary categories of planer — the portable and the stationary — and two price ranges: under $450 and over $450 (often, way over). Now, you can find a planer that fits on a bench top, and can be lifted off and stored — albeit with two hands. You also can find a planer that sits on its own stand and will work all day, every day, turning out smoothed, sized wood for all your projects. The smaller planers are not all-day, every-day, tools, but will surface and size many hundreds, even thousands, of board feet annually without complaint. There are also planer-molders that offer the ability to add molding knives to the cutterheads. These may offer slightly differing cut widths.

Ridgid's TP1300 13" benchtop planer offers double-sided disposable blades, locking head and material-removal gauge.

Understanding the Features

Beds

Beds are of great importance. They must be smoothly finished and are best kept well-waxed to reduce hang-ups. One option is planers with or without bed rollers. Some manufacturers contend that bed rollers aren't necessary for smaller planers. Your opinion may differ.

Magnetic Switches

Some stationary planers offer magnetic switches, a good safety feature that shuts the machine down if power fails. (Standard switches stay on when power fails, which means the tool starts running as soon as power is turned back on.)

Feed Rollers

Feed rollers are the part of the machine that pulls the lumber past the cutter knives, and can be either hard rubber or serrated steel. Whole-steel feed rollers give more positive "traction"; the rubber rollers work adequately and keep the cost of portable units down.

Top Rollers

Top rollers are available on some larger planers and are a good feature that allow the operator to feed planed stock back to the incoming end so the other side can be fed, or another pass can be made.

Knife-Setting Gauges

Knife-setting gauges are included with most planers. You'll almost certainly be buying a special gauge at some point, though most factory models are fine to start with.

Feed Rate

The feed rate is the number of feet per minute the stock is pulled through the machine. Most portable planers have two-knife cutterheads, so that an 8000-rpm universal motor offers 16,000 cuts per minute. The more cuts per minute, the smoother the final finish on the stock will be, if knives are sharp and cut depth is light.

Portable Planers

Portable planers are the low-cost, small-shop alternative, and seldom weigh more than 80 pounds, while offering as much as a 13" planing width. Lighter models are available at weights of about 50 pounds. Evolutionary changes have led to the smaller planers sharing many features larger machines have had for a long time. Two-knife cutterheads spin at great speed and rubber-coated feed rollers pass the work along the cutterheads (rubber-coated rollers have to be replaced at intervals, depending on their wear).

Portable planers generally have between 12- and 13"-width capacity these days. Cut width is determined by the length of the blades, which affects infeed and outfeed tables and feed roller widths — so the widest stock you can thickness is used as the ultimate capacity of the planer.

Portable planers may offer quick-change disposable blades or double-edged reversible blades to save "down" time. Both of these may add to overall blade expense, it is usually minor, under $50 a year.

Thickness and Cut-Depth Capacity

Cut depth on portable planers is a maximum of ⅛". Material thickness may be up to 6", with a minimum of ⅛". The minimum stock length is usually around 12", which is the shortest length which can be safely fed across the knives.

Power

Portable planers all use universal motors which run on 115 volts, but require a 20-amp circuit with nothing else on it or, at the very least, nothing else running when the planer is in operation.

Cutterhead Support

The newest generation of portable planers offers several features that are worth having. Probably foremost is a feature that has existed on some models for several years — the use of four posts to support the cutterhead. Using four posts reduces cutterhead rocking during operation, which, therefore, reduces snipe.

Snipe is a possible problem with any jointer or planer, but was a serious problem with early portable planers. Snipe is a cupping cut at the start or end of a board as it wobbles vertically through the cutterhead (or as the cutterhead wobbles). Lightweight infeed

JET's model JPM-13 planer offers quality planing features and also will function as a molder.

The Delta model 22-560 benchtop planer offers many worthwhile features for an affordable price.

Tip *Dust hoods are not standard equipment with all planers. Get one. A dust hood is a "don't leave home without it" necessity for planers — machines that produce the largest piles of chips and sawdust of any woodworking tool, and do it fast. The dust hood must, of course, connect to a dust collector. Prices vary depending on planer size, but most 15" models should have hoods available for $40 or so.*

tor is a better idea. It will also keep your shop from getting buried in a pile of poplar or walnut!

Price
The price range of portable planers is reasonable: low-price models are around $300, while most top-price models are about $450. There is a planer-molder in the portable category that sells for about $650, while a portable jointer-planer could cost up to $1100.

In Portable Planers, Look For:
- Sturdy construction, with easy-to-open handles and a solid base.
- Smooth bed, with a very fine finish.
- Well-finished and easily adjustable infeed and outfeed tables or rollers.
- Ease and precision of vertical head movement.
- Generally good fit and finish (the less you pay, the less good fit and finish will be).
- Locking head. If there is no head lock, look for an adjustment wheel or handle on top of the saw where vibration has less effect on settings.
- 2-hp motor is preferable, but check for 15 amps on the label.
- Ease of blade changing.
- Four posts.
- The ability to incorporate dust collection.
- Capacity — does it meet your needs?
- Weight — will you be able to lift it off the bench?

MOBILE BASES

For stationary planers in smaller shops, a mobile base is exceptionally handy. Especially on 15" planers, prices are reasonable — from as low as $70 plus shipping, and it's incredibly useful.

As the planer grows in size and weight, the mobile base does as well. Prices correlate with this size increase, but 1200-pound mobile bases can still be bought for about $100 and up.

---

and outfeed tables, as well as inadequate cutterhead support, create snipe problems. By using four support posts instead of two, cutterhead support is doubled and rocking is less likely. Add heavy-duty infeed and outfeed tables or rollers that are adjustable for height, and snipe is reduced even more.

Cutterhead Locks
The newest portable planers have added another feature to help reduce

snipe — the cutterhead lock. This mechanism applies pressure against the support parts to fix the cutterhead in its present location. This feature is mostly used during the last pass on a side to remove any pre-existing snipe. While not foolproof, the cutterhead lock does improve finish.

Turret Adjustment
Turret adjustments for sizes most often used allow you to easily return to a size, so if not enough stock is planed at the first session, you can use the turret adjustment and plane to an identical thickness the next time around. Turret thickness adjustments are still available on only a few portable planers.

Dust Collection
More than any other tool, planers make chips and dust. The removal of these chips can be very important. Most portable planers include a dust port, or have one available as an accessory. While most of these will blow the chips away from the machine, a dust collec-

Stationary Planers

The stationary planer is more powerful, much heavier and more effective with heavier stock. It is also more likely to survive day-in, day-out use.

Stationary planers generally start at 12" capacity. Stock thickness and thinness capacities vary little at this point. As the machine's capacity increases to 15" and 20", thickness capacities change, as well. At least one 24" commercial planer accepts material as thick as 9⅜", and will lay in a maximum depth cut, at full width, of almost half an inch. This unit more than meets either the needs or capacities of a small shop (using three-phase electricity and weighing 1675 pounds, it would stress even some commercial shops). Single-phase 24" planers are also available, but the cost approaches $4000 and they weigh over half a ton.

For most practical purposes, the 15" stationary planer remains the most popular in small shops. Several makers produce models that offer strong features, including variable feed rates (usually 16 fpm × 20 fpm), good power and a moderately heavy overall weight (which absorbs vibration). Cutterheads take three knives and turn at about 3800 to 5000 rpm, thus yielding 13,000 to 15,000 cuts per minute, which gives a very smooth finish. If you do a lot of wide panels or wide-board work, consider planers from 18" to 20" in capacity. Less costly models are priced at about $1300, and weight from 420 to 920 pounds.

Induction v. Universal

All the stationary planers use induction motors, which are more durable, powerful and considerably quieter than universal motors. But just because stationary planers are quieter than the portable planers does NOT mean that you should use these machines without hearing protection. Regardless of motor type, the planer is the king of racket in the woodworking shop and requires efficient hearing protection.

Feed Rollers

Unlike the rubber-coated feed rollers of the benchtop models, feed rollers for stationary planers are usually made of serrated steel. The serrations run longitudinally, or twist around the roller. They are far more durable than their rubber-covered counterparts, but precise adjustment is essential to prevent marking the stock.

Thickness and Cut-Depth Capacity

Most 15" stationary planers have a stock thickness capacity of around 6", while cut depth may run anywhere from 3/32" up to 1/4". Cut depths remain close to 1/4" with wider planers, though one or two are designed to hog off as much as 5/16".

Grizzly's 15" stationary planer, model G10212, offers professional-level capacity at a home-shop price.

Bridgewood's 20" stationary planer, model BW-200P, is able to handle boards up to 20" wide at a price that will still let you afford nicely figured lumber.

Planer-Molders

Planer-molders are a small segment of the planer industry, with probably 10 versions available in different brands, besides the single portable version. Most planer-molders are 12½" to 13" capacity for planing width, and will cut up to about 4½"-wide molding. Knife setup in most can take 15 minutes, but there is at least one model that accepts knives without any adjustment needed for two or three minutes. The cost per inch of planing width is always higher with planer-molders. Power is not a whole lot higher than portable planers, until you start looking at models that cost up to $1000.

Pricing

Prices for stationary planers start around $700, and rise to over $3900. Most models are clustered in the $800 to $1100 price ranges. Power varies between 2 or 3 hp, and weigh from 395 to 700 pounds (the 700-pounder is the largest and one of the most expensive, but it does have two motors). Almost all have three-knife cutterheads; cutterhead speed is around 5000 rpm (the lowest speed is 4500, the highest single-motor speed is 6500 — but the 6500 is on a two-knife cutterhead).

In Stationary Planers, Look For:

- Sturdy construction with plenty of cast iron for less vibration.
- Smooth bed, with a very fine finish.
- Strongly constructed infeed and outfeed rollers or tables.
- Easily accessible rollers, both infeed and outfeed.
- Generally good fit and finish (the less you pay, the poorer the fit and finish will be).
- Easily operated controls for adjusting cut depth.
- How easily does the lock mechanism, if there is one, work?
- Easily reached chains for drive system.
- Oil-bath drive system (larger models, 15" and up).
- 230-volt motor.
- A dust collection port — anything

RBI planer-molder, model 812.

under 4" is too small.
- Sturdy stand or cabinet.
- Four posts.
- Cutterhead speed.
- Switchable feed rate.
- How easy is it to change and adjust blades? How costly are sets of new blades?
- Capacity — does it meet your needs?
- What is the weight and can you get it into place without damage to yourself, friends, floors, vehicles or friendships?

The Coin Flip:

For many home woodworkers, a 12- to 13" portable planer will meet many of their needs. There are half a dozen machines available which are very close in performance and price. Look for more to come. If you are using wider lumber, highly figured species or just running a lot of rough stock, invest in a good 15" planer. The cost is more than double sometimes, but the benefits will offset the price.

PLANER-PAL

Planers don't need or accept many accessories, but a generally useful one that can save hours is a device know as a Planer-Pal. These are knife-setting jigs that reset planer knives to an accuracy of .002 inches.

In essence, Planer-Pals hold the knives magnetically, while you reset them as needed — saving cuts, nicked knives and similar problems, as well as out-of-adjustment knives that mess up wood.

Depending on features, knife holders can cost from $60 a set up to $200.

tools | **routers**

You want a router if you plan to edge a simple or complex project in any of hundreds of styles. You want a router if you're going to make signs that require internal design or cuts. You want a router if you want to make molding in any of thousands of types or patterns. You want a router if you want to use jigs to make dovetailed or finger-jointed projects.

A router also works, with templates, for hollowing out solid wood seats and trays, producing duplicate parts from patterns, making raised panels, making cope-and-stile panel frames for cabinetry, for ... OK, you don't *want* a router. You *need* a router.

The standard router is a motor with a collet (similar in performance, if not in exact appearance, to a drill chuck) on one end and a base attached around the barrel. Some form of switch controls power and the collet holds a bit in place. The bit is inserted and tightened in the collet, the router is placed against or on the work. When the switch is turned on, the bit cuts into the work surface, providing — one hopes — the pattern needed. Various jigs help assure that the work is completed as desired. The router may have more jigs designed and made for it than any other tool — except possibly the table saw.

What's Out There

The router began as a hand tool. Power was added by R. L. Carter in 1919. By 1929, the portable, powered router was in production. That same year, Stanley bought out the original developers. Since that time, the router has contin-

Black & Decker's router (left), model RT5200, is the economy plunge-router option for hobbyists, while the Festo (far left), model F 1000 E, is designed and priced for professional woodworkers.

ued to increase in popularity and, today, many small-shop woodworkers aren't comfortable with fewer than three routers. Today's electric router accepts bits with shank diameters from ¼" to ½", in several hundred patterns (thousands if you count minor variations).

There are numerous base plate styles, switch styles, overall shapes, accessory availability and other features, including fixed and plunge bases. Motor speeds on routers vary from as low as 8000 rpm on an adjustable speed router, to as high as 26,000 rpm

on a full-size router. Variable speeds let you match speed to router-bit size (the bigger the bit's cutting diameter, the slower the speed you use) and wood density and hardness. Some routers are intended as single-use types, such as laminate trimmers, while others are made for every possible use, such as plunge routers.

Routers can also be mounted in router tables to make it easier to run a lot of one edge profile, or to make it safer to move smaller pieces of wood past the bit. Both plunge or fixed-base routers can be used in a router table.

Understanding the Features

Speed Controls

Some form of speed control is essential when using larger router bits. There are routers with several speeds, selectable by switch, while there are others with EVS (electronic variable speed). EVS allows setting a desired speed on a dial, usually with infinite adjustment within its range. EVS is a good option.

Collet Sizes And Bit Shanks

The most common collet sizes in U.S.-sold routers are ¼", ⅜" and ½". The two end sizes, ¼" and ½", are by far the most popular. Metric sizes are also available, most often 8 mm, usually as sleeves to fit inside the ½" collet (the ⅜" size is often a sleeve, too). They may be needed to fit bits that work with particular jigs. Collet size determines the shank size of the bits you may use. In general, the thicker shank is better because there is less deflection possible in heavy cutting. But that thicker shank comes with a heavier bit using more material and needing more machining, which means higher cost. Because router bits eventually (and, actually, fairly quickly) become much more of an expense than the router itself, you will want some lighter shank bits for light-duty edging and similar decorative jobs where side-to-side stresses are not great and fit is less critical than, for example, dovetails in a drawer.

Work Lights

Some routers have work lights. These are sometimes handy, but not essential, items. If you can, use a router with a work light and one without and see if the light makes any difference in your comfort level.

Spindle Locks

Most routers require two wrenches to change a bit, but more and more manufacturers are offering a spindle lock, which requires only one wrench. This is a great feature, and until wrenches are obsolete, it makes changing bits much easier.

Pricing

Routers run from a low of under $70 to more than $500. Forget the really low-price models unless you have no other choice. Good mid-range routers with ⅞ horsepower and up will start at about $180 and rise to about $350. Make your selection in that range. Good laminate trimmers start at about $100 and rise to about $200 for kits with several bases. There are several reasons for selecting laminate trimmers, but low price is not one, because capacities are noticeably lower than with regular routers — though prices may not be.

Laminate Trimmers

Laminate trimmers are the lightweights of the category, though they can do yeoman service as one hand routers, as well as trimming laminate to whatever angle your job needs. These small, slender units are available with different types of bases that include a straight-locked base, an offset base and a tilt base. Kits may include a power unit, case and two or three different bases. Most are around 5 or 6 amps in power, with ¼" collets, spindle locks and exceptionally high speeds, often in the 30,000 rpm range.

In Routers, Look For:

- Good feel in your hand.
- Generally good fit and finish: name brands all have good fit and finish.
- Does it have the style base you need?
- Useful speed range for your needs.
- Is the base easy to adjust for height?
- Is the switch easy to reach?
- What is the weight? Anything too heavy would be unwieldy when working with delicate laminates.

WRENCHLESS COLLET

The wave of the future is a wrenchless collet for routers. Not unlike the keyless chuck for drills, two companies currently offer after-market replacement collets which allow you to throw away the wrenches. There are currently some trade-offs in using these accessories, but anticipate a wrenchless-router world in the next few years.

The Bosch 1609AK trimmer kit offers a versatile ¼" collet router with standard base, offset base and beveling base for around $200.

Fixed-Base Routers

Fixed-base routers are stars for much routing work; they come in just about every power and handle pattern any router does. Lighter routers such as ¾ hp, 1 hp and 1½ hp, are easier to handle, no matter the handle configuration. Depending on actual power and product quality, motors on fixed-base routers under 1½ hp will be about 8 amps, sometimes a little less. In general, for serious long-term woodworking, it is better to begin at 1½ hp. Such routers are available in two-knob (knobs on each side of the base plate) design and D-handle design (more easily controlled, with the switch right by the thumb or forefinger; knob handles force you to take your hand off one handle to operate the switch). Rpm for these routers may reach 26,000, and speed controls that give rpm ranges, for example, from 8,000 to 25,000 are available.

Power

Fixed-base routers with larger motors are also available, with advertised horsepower of 2, 3 and even 3¼. As power increases, so does router size and weight. A 1½-hp knob-handled router may weigh 8 pounds. The same company's 3-hp router weighs over 17 pounds, more than twice as much! For heavy work, and for use in router tables, the big, powerful routers get down there and grunt, and will do it on a day-in, day-out basis unapproachable by lighter-duty machinery.

Porter-Cable's router, model 693PK, includes a 1½-hp router motor with both a fixed base and a plunge base. This is a great starter router for any woodworker.

In Fixed-Base Routers, Look For:

- Is there a sturdy feel, plenty of heft to reduce the effects of vibration?
- Good feel in your hand.
- Generally good fit and finish: name brands all have good fit and finish.
- Useful speed range for your needs. Single-speed works fine for most small bits. Multi-speed models are best for larger bits. Check for switched speeds or EVS.
- If a high horsepower model, does it have a soft startup?
- Type of speed control (dial or switch to specific speed).
- Does it take collets to ½" capacity? Acceptance of only ¼" shank bits reduces utility.
- Does it have a flat top? A flat top lets the router stand on its top while you change bits, making the job easier.
- Easty-to-hook-up dust collection port (most have none)?
- Is the fixed base easy to adjust for height?
- Is the switch easy to reach?
- What is the weight? You want a hefty feel, without excess weight. Weights of 3-hp models vary as much as 6 pounds. Lighter models need to weigh at least 6 or 7 pounds. Anything lighter feels flighty and uncontrollable.

ROUTER TABLES

The router table is the ultimate starter jig for the router. It provides a stable work surface that allows you to add jigs and procedures to make box joints, raised panels, cope-and-stick joinery for the rails and stiles to hold the panels and a slew of other items. You can make your own router table, starting from scratch, including the insert to hold the router in place, or you can buy a completed table from any of at least a half-dozen commercial builders. You may also build your own leg set and install a commercial top; build your own top and install a commercial leg set; build everything but the fence; build the fence and buy everything else; or any other stop along the way. In the end, you will have a tool that will do many jobs well, especially if you have built and bought wisely. You can build a router table for the cost of the wood and the laminate and a few knobs, or you can spend as much as $400 for a commercial unit (without a router).

Plunge-Base Routers

Plunge routers' heads mount on two posts that are part of the base. The router is placed on the work and pressed down, forcing the bit into the work at a 90-degree angle. Plunge bases are a fairly recent development for routers, and for a few years (not too long ago) were considered the "hot" setup, supplanting the fixed-base router, or about to do so.

The changeover never totally took place for several reasons. First, until recently, plunge-base routers were the larger, heavier workhorses of the line, and few people feel a need for that much weight and power. Possibly more important, plunge-base routers wear out slightly faster than those with fixed bases because the shafts on which the router plunges and the bearing surfaces that ride on those shafts, are liable to wear. Any tool that has more parts is harder to keep going than a simpler tool. Plunge routers are superb, though, where they are needed. In making interior cuts for mortises, stopped dadoes or any operation where the router needs to start its own hole, the safety factor is increased, as are the convenience and accuracy.

Many plunge routers also offer plunge stops, turret-style depth stops that let you plunge to different depths in a single job without having to back out and reset the depth each time. Zero the router and set the first depth. Set the second depth. And so on. Start the job as needed and use the setting needed for each part. A handy feature on some jobs, and never in the way when it's not needed. A related cousin is the fine-depth adjustment on some routers, offering variable depths of .001".

You want to consider plunge depth possibilities, too. If you're never going to be cutting deep mortises, you may not need the 3" plunge capacity offered by a number of routers, but you need to be sure you can get by with the 2" plunge depth offered by others.

DeWalt's DW621 plunge-base router is a versatile and user-friendly router with dust collection.

Porter-Cable's 7519 3¼-hp router is a great choice for use in a router table, providing plenty of power for the most demanding tasks.

Power

Again, power is a wide option, with plunge routers starting at 1¼ hp and going up to 3½ hp. And, just as before, more power means more weight and bulk. Large routers, though, work exceptionally well in router tables where they can be used to form raised panels or other items that need lots of wood taken off in a single pass (though at least two passes should be made to assure a fine finish cut).

Make sure those whacking great motors, 2 hp and up, have soft start, if you can. These small universal motors kick out an interesting amount of torque on start up, as they scream almost instantly to their top speed of 20,000 to 25,000 rpm. It's nice to not have to fight that torque every time you squeeze the trigger or flick the switch. And it's safer, too, because even the strongest of us can be caught unaware from time to time — causing that unprotected, rapidly rotating bit to move around in unplanned ways. Soft-start eliminates that, or nearly so.

In Plunge-Base Routers, Look For:

- Is there a sturdy feel, plenty of heft to reduce the effects of vibration?
- Good feel in your hand.
- Generally good fit and finish: name brands all have good fit and finish.
- Useful speed range for your needs. Single-speed works fine for most small bits. Multi-speed models are best for larger bits. Check for switched speeds or EVS.
- If a high horsepower model, does it have a soft startup?
- Type of speed control (dial or switch to specific speed).
- Does it take collets to $\frac{1}{2}$" capacity?
- Does it have a flat top? A flat top lets the router stand on its top while you change bits, making the job easier.
- Easy-to-hook-up dust collection port (most have none).
- Are plunge controls easy to use?
- Is the plunge lock positive?
- Is the depth control easy to set (plunge routers)?
- Is the depth turret control easy to adjust?
- Does the depth turret control stay on setting with slippage?
- Is the switch easy to reach?
- What is the weight? You want a hefty feel, without excess weight. Weights of 3-hp models vary as much as 6 pounds. Lighter models need to weigh at least 6 or 7 pounds. Anything lighter feels flighty and uncontrollable.

The Coin Flip:

Look at the work you have to do. If it's all light-duty stuff, mostly edge trimming and some veining or work with core-box bits, then any 1-hp router of decent construction that feels good in your hands will probably do. If you're planning more work and deeper cuts

ROTARY TOOLS

They may be small, but there's not much you can't do with them, if you set your mind to it. Rotary tools are miniature powerhouses. Dremel, by far, is the best-known name, and the originator of, this type of tool.

It's a very versatile tool. Combined with any of dozens of types of bits, flexible shafts, mounting platforms and other accessories, rotary tools can tackle jobs that no other power tool will even consider. By using the fiberglass cut-off wheels, you can cut through the toughest materials quickly. Or attach a sanding drum or polishing bonnet, and produce a fine finish in a tight spot. It can be used for everything from cutting off a rusted-in-place 2" ball hitch on a truck, to boring tiny holes in models. You can switch bits and engrave glass or carve wood. Rotary tools aren't usually tools you call on every day. They're specialists ... summoned when nothing else in your workshop arsenal has a fighting chance. And for close-quarters work, there's nothing to compare.

There are three types of rotary tools, although the differences are subtle. Most common is the typical, handheld, Dremel-style, high-speed tool — either cordless or corded. Typically, speeds run from around 5,000 rpm to 30,000 rpm, with multiple settings in between. Most of these are barrel-shaped bodies and are thin enough to be held either like a pen or by the barrel. You'll also find a few brands offering more of a pistol-grip shape.

Hanging models use a flexible shaft connected to the motor, which is suspended from a hook or bracket above your workbench. The flexible shaft gives you a smaller tool end — the part you hold — allowing you to get the bit into tighter spots. This is best controlled by a foot switch, which is usually offered as an option. These types are the preferred choice of carvers and modelmakers. Hanging models usually offer less rpm than their handheld brothers do. Note that the conventional hand-held models can have a flex shaft added, and be hung from a hook. There are some rotary tools that don't fit any particular niche. The Roto-Zip is one example — it's a re-modeler's tool that is larger and more powerful. Think of it as a router for carpenters, aimed at making openings for plumbing and wiring in wallboard, stucco, plaster and plywood. Also found are specialized pneumatic (air-powered) die grinders that spin at 60,000 rpm, as well as wood-carving systems that rely on a reciprocating saw action.

over a longer period of time, go with a better quality 1½-hp or even a 2-hp unit. If you want a plunge router, consider your needs. For most work, you'll probably be just as satisfied with a fixed-base router, but if you do intend internal cuts or sign making, then a plunge router is handy, as it is when you make lots of mortises and similar joint cut.

If you're expecting to use a router table, then start thinking at 2 hp and go on from there. It is in the router table that the big routers really shine. You

have a good selection, from 2 hp up to past 3 hp, with lots of features and a great price variation, so get used to the look and feel of several of the big routers. Some routers are designed for use in router tables, where their inverted position allows dust to enter the machine. These routers have fans, or cases, designed for dust intrusion.

If you want both handheld use and a router table, look into the possibility of buying at least two routers — a lightweight one for handheld work and a "monster" for table use.

Choosing the Best Router Bit

There are thousands of router bits available today from dozens of reputable manufacturers. In general, most are quality products that will provide you with good performance. Quality of the bit isn't something that's immediately obvious while shopping, though. Only by using the bit is the quality evident. There are, however, a few things you should know about router bits which will help you choose a bit that will meet your needs.

Sets or Not?

The router bit question heard most often is should you buy a router bit set or buy bits as needed? Buying bits individually is the most practical option. By purchasing bits as you need them, you build a set that accurately reflects your needs. Yes, most sets offer bits that you will likely use in the future, but what if the set includes a ¼" roundover when you really want a ⅜" roundover? Back to the store. Your decision should come down to economics. If you can afford to buy bits for the future, great. If you're doing your woodworking on today's paycheck, buy what you need as you go. If you've wisely followed the advice in the router section of this book, your router will accept both ¼" and ½" shanked bits. So given the option, what bits should you buy in what shank size? In general, ½" shanks are preferable as they provide a more stable cut, but can be more expensive. So choose a sensible mix. A number of cutter shapes are small enough (¼" roundovers, veining bits, small chamfer bits) to give good performance with ¼" shanks. Buy these bits in ¼" and buy your larger bits in ½" shank.

HSS or Carbide?

Bits can be purchased in either high-speed steel HSS or carbide. Carbide bits can be found as a solid carbide cut-

An integral pin-guided bit (far left, note the burned surface of the pin), a non-guided bit, center, and on the right, a bearing-guided bit.

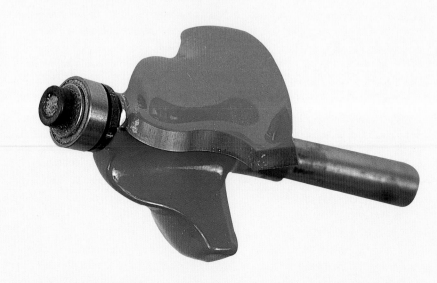

The anti-kickback design offers a much smaller gullet space to avoid anything being trapped between the wings. The extra material also improves the stability of the cut.

ter, or as a steel blank with a carbide tip brazed in place. In general, high-speed steel bits are not designed for longevity. They tend to be sold as "starter" bits, or single-use bits. Even though carbide bits are more expensive than steel bits, whenever possible, choose carbide. They hold a sharp cut-

ting edge longer than steel bits and will perform better on highly figured woods. Carbide bits do require specialized sharpening processes most woodworkers can't do, while steel can be sharpened by the home woodworker if required. That isn't a good enough reason to buy high-speed steel bits.

One Flute or Two?

Bits are sold in two basic configurations, with either a single flute (or cutting surface) or a double-flute option. The single-flute design is an economy bit, with the double-flute bit being the more expensive option, but the finish of the cut reflects the expense. The double-flute design offers twice as many cuts as a single flute in the same amount of time, thus improving the smoothness of the finish. As an added benefit, the double-flute bits provide a better finish with slower (below 22,000 rpm) routers.

Straight, Shear And Spiral

Beyond the one- or two-flute option, bits are available in straight, shear and spiral designs. Shear cutters have slightly angled flutes to provide a paring motion that reduces wear on the tool, and also offers a cleaner cut in end grain or figured woods with less tear-out. The shear bits also provide improved waste removal, again reducing wear on the tool and bit. Straight- or shear-cutting bits are often sold with guide bearings and are designed for pattern routing, edge smoothing, and (without a bearing guide) limited plunge routing for mortises and grooves.

Spiral cutters, (made of solid carbide rather than brazed carbide flutes) are designed for mortising, grooving and inlay work. They are available as either upward or downward spiral cutters. Upward cutting bits provide excellent waste removal while providing an aggressive shearing cut and a very clean surface on the exit side of a through mortise. Downward cutting bits offer improved edge finish and give a very clean surface on the entrance side of a through mortise, though waste removal requires a slower pace. If choosing between solid carbide spiral bits, and brazed carbide straight bits, you will need to consider price vs. use.

A wide variety of profile and joinery bits from Bosch.

Solid carbide bits can be five times as expensive as carbide-tipped bits, so make sure you need the benefit of a solid carbide bit.

Bearing Guides

Some edge-profile bits (such as rabbeting and roundover bits), are for sale with or without a guide. The bits without a guide are designed to be used with a fence attached to the router base. The guided bits will use either an integral (fixed) guide pin or a ball-bearing guide. Integral guide pins are cheaper, but they can burn the edge of the work; bearing guides offer a clean and easy cut, and also offer the choice of changing the size of the bearing to adjust the cut profile without buying a new bit. We recommend bearing-guided profile bits whenever affordable. If you want to use them with a router-mounted guide, that option is still available.

Why Are Some Bits So Cheap?

When pricing different bits you may find very similar cutting designs with widely varying prices. Some of this price difference may be due to the quality of the carbide used. Another price factor is the increasing (and smart) use of anti-kickback designs. These bits have beefy bodies behind the cutting flutes that limit the amount of space between each flute. This design provides a more stable and a safer cut, and the extra material also dissipates heat, improving the life of the bit.

Jigs, Jigs, Jigs

Cutting dovetails is one of the premier jobs of the router, and three jigs top the scale for utility or ease of use. There are literally dozens of lesser jigs out there that can do the job, often not as easily or as well, but for far less money.

Two router bits and a dovetail jig can let the average mildly experienced woodworker turn out professional-looking drawers or other box-style projects with reasonable rapidity and great accuracy (with most such jigs, time of setup and difficulty of setup present such a learning curve that it's easier to learn to cut dovetails by hand for projects that need only a few drawers or boxes).

scroll saws

In many woodworkers' minds, the scroll saw isn't a real woodworking tool. It seems to be the tool of choice for a number of craft applications, but its use in a woodworking shop isn't obvious. It's true, a scroll saw is an excellent tool for a wide variety of craft and hobby projects. But if you've ever looked at a Chinese Chippendale table and appreciated the intricately pierced gallery rails, you've found a very serious woodworking application for a scroll saw. Inlays, fretwork and intarsia all benefit from the very unique abilities of a scroll saw.

What's Out There

Scroll saws have come a long way in the past few years. Traditionally available either in a high-end ($1,000 or more) professional model, or as a reasonably inexpensive (around $200) tool that worked adequately for weekend crafters, a number of mid-priced tools have been added to the market. These mid-range scroll saws include many of the best features of the higher-priced models in a $500-or-less price range.

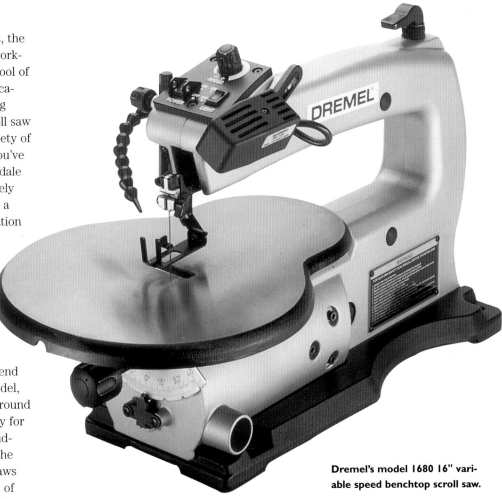

Dremel's model 1680 16" variable speed benchtop scroll saw.

Understanding the Features

Variable Speed

Some wood types cut better at lower speed settings, while some blades and cutting applications can also benefit from variable speeds. If you expect to be working primarily in pine and producing fairly simple patterns, the variable speed feature may not be worth the extra money.

Size

The size of the scroll saw is determined by the throat capacity from the base of the arm to the blade. This size is important as it limits the width and length of the workpiece able to be cut on the saw, ranging generally from 12" capacity in the less expensive models up to 30" in the professional models. Again, your use of the tool will determine what size saw is your best purchase.

Arm Design

There are three scroll-saw arm designs available on the market today. The type of arm design that's best for you will, again, depend on your type of work. Parallel arm designs move the blade in a straight up-and-down action providing a very clean cut, which is good for fine and tight radius work. The C-arm action moves the blade in a slight forward-and-back arc, which provides a more aggressive cut, but can also reduce the turning radius and leave a rougher cut. The link arm design actually still creates a parallel arm motion, but with only part of the arm moving. The arms shift forward and backward slightly to compensate for the slight orbital action, maintaining a straight up-and-down motion for tight radius cutting. In addition, since only part of the arm is moving, there is less vibration in the machine, providing a more stable and user-friendly tool.

Blade Release

Unlike a jigsaw or band saw, much scroll-saw work uses inside cuts which require you to drill a clearance hole through the wood, then thread the blade through the hole. This means you end up detaching and reattaching the

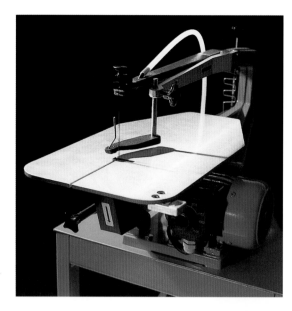

Hegner's Multicut-1 precision scroll saw; Hegner's first hobby-line scroll saw.

DeWalt's DW788 is a link arm design 20" variable speed scroll saw.

blade a number of times during a fretwork project. Scroll saws are available with blade releases that either require a screwdriver or hex-head wrench to change the blade, a thumb screw release, or a pressure-clamping system that doesn't require any tools. It's hard to imagine a situation where you would choose a blade-release system that requires a tool over the "non-tool" variety. The price for a scroll saw with a pressure-clamping release system (usually found on the mid- to upper-range saws) may make that option more difficult, but a thumb screw isn't very expensive.

Blower

Another recommended feature for any extended scroll-saw work is a blower that forces air across the work surface to move dust out of the way of the cut. Standard on a lot of scroll saws in every price range, some saws may not

have this option. It may seem inconsequential, but when you start making dust, the blower is a nice feature.

Two Foot Options

The hold-down foot can be a blessing or a hindrance. In most cases, a well-designed hold-down is the best bet. It should provide enough pressure to keep the material from sliding on its own with the machine vibration, but be flexible enough to allow you to move the piece without pushing too hard. It should also swing out of the way without too much trouble during cuts when it is less desirable.

Another foot consideration is a strongly recommended accessory. A foot pedal to operate the saw allows you immediate control of the saw, without moving your hand from the work. This is a safer procedure, allows a great deal more control and is generally a very nice option.

In Scroll Saws, Look For:

- Toolless blade change.
- Easily accessible controls.
- Sturdy construction, better height, more stable cut.
- Preferred arm style.
- Convenient material hold-down
- Variable speed.
- Foot-controlled on/off switch.
- Table size and throat size that meet your needs.

The Coin Flip:

Start your shopping by deciding what needs you have for a scroll saw. If you are ready to add fretwork or intarsia to your already impressive array of woodworking skills, or if you plan to dedicate the majority of your woodworking time to produce a lot of scroll-sawn craft items, you'll want to consider the mid- to high-end tool. If, on the other hand, you see the scroll saw as a nice tool to have around every now and then, you may put your needs in the less expensive category.

Recommended Blades Scroll Saws

For very intricate cutting in wood thicknesses of $1/16"$ to $3/32"$:

no. 2/0 (28 tpi), 0 (25 tpi), 1 (23 tpi)

For tight turns in materials $3/32"$ to $1/8"$:

no. 2 (20 tpi), no. 3 (18 tpi), no. 4 (15 tpi)

For tight turns in $1/8"$ or thicker material:

no. 5 (14 tpi), no. 5 (13 tpi)

Common blade for hard and soft woods from $3/16"$ to 2" thick:

no. 7 (12 tpi)
no. 8 (11.5 tpi)
no. 9 (11.5, thicker and wider blade)
no. 10 (11 tpi)
no. 11 (9.5 tpi)
no. 12 (9.5, thicker and wider blade)

BLADES

Like most other cutting tools, a scroll saw provides the best service when outfitted with the right blade for the individual job. But before discussing the wide variety of teeth configurations, let's start at the ends of the blade. Two types of blade are sold for scroll saws: pin-end and plain-end blades. Pin-end blades have a short metal pin running across the end of the blade, perpendicular to its length. Plain-end blades don't have this pin. Pin-end blades fit in and out of standard blade holders on the saw without need of tools to loosen the holder. However, the fixed pin at the end of the blade makes it a poor choice for fine fretwork, as the end of the blade will not fit through very small clearance holes. So while they're more trouble to change and adjust, plain-end blades are more versatile.

Concerning teeth configuration and orientation, choosing the correct blade will depend on your saw type, the material and the thickness you are cutting. Also important is the complexity of the cuts you are making, the cutting speed of the saw and the required edge-finish of the cut. Scroll saw blades are offered with teeth-per-inch, then by tooth orientation, with skip tooth, reverse-skip tooth, double-skip tooth, spiral and precision-ground as options. See chart for the most efficient use of each blade design.

As with table saw blades, the more teeth on the blade, the smoother the finish on the material. For the most efficient blade performance, three teeth should be touching the wood at all times. So, if you're cutting a 1"-thick piece of pine, in general a 3-tpi blade will work well. For $1/2"$ material, use 6 tpi.

A thinner blade, called a fret blade, is used for more delicate work and complicated designs. Not only is the fret blade thinner, but it uses a skip-tooth design to let sawdust clear away from the kerf. This produces a better cut and lets the blade stay sharp longer. One variation to the basic fret blade — a reverse-tooth blade — is a fret blade which has the teeth at the bottom of the blade, cutting on the upward stroke. This helps to provide a cleaner cut on both sides of the material with less tearout. One premium feature in scroll saw blades are precision-ground blades. These blades are ground to cut equally on each side of the blade, offering a much cleaner cut. They're more expensive, but in fine detail work they pay for themselves.

Another blade option is the spiral blade. Designed for very tight turns, the blades are twisted to allow the teeth to cut in all directions. These blades are especially useful when making beveled cuts, when turning the piece during the cut would change the bevel of the cut.

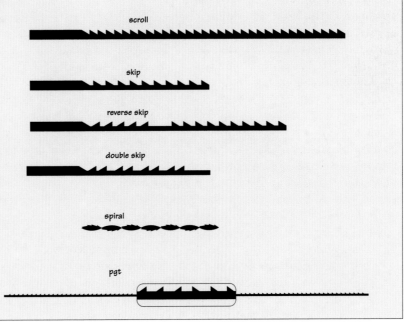

scroll

skip

reverse skip

double skip

spiral

pgt

tools | **sanders**

Sanding is everyone's least favorite part of woodworking, but you can't say you don't have a lot of powerful help to get it done. A few good sanders can turn the drudgery into ... well, not fun exactly, but at least a bit easier than usual.

Sanders are actually rather creative woodworking tools. You can flatten surfaces, shape wood, create perfect joints and angles, polish parts and deliver a final few thousand strokes in preparation for applying a finish. Some sanders do specialized jobs very well, but no sander can do them all. For true sanding efficiency, you need a selection of sanders — each aimed at completing a specific task.

What's Out There
You could write a book about sanders — there are simply so many styles, models and brands available. (For detailed information about pneumatic sanders, please see the "Air Tools" section.) Here are the categories you'll encounter:

Random Orbit Sanders
Random orbit sanders have round sanding pads, which move in a random, orbital pattern (hence the name). They remove material fairly rapidly, and because of the random motion, leave very few marks on the finished surface.

Detail Sanders
These are the sanders you turn to for tight corners and oddball shapes. Detail sanders belong to a newer breed of tool you won't use as often as other models, but they're tremendous time, frustration and finger savers.

Fein Multimaster detail sander.

Belt Sanders
Belt sanders are the wood-chomping hogs of the sander world. They rely on speed, coarse grits and cutting area to remove a lot of material quickly. They're also the quickest way to turn a project into firewood if you're not paying attention.

Oscillating Spindle Sanders
The oscillating spindle sander has been around a long time, but only recently have they been priced for the small woodshop. A spindle, set in the center of a small table, oscillates up and down as it spins. Rpm is usually around 200, while up and down strokes move at 60 per minute.

Stationary Belt/Disc Sanders
These stand-mounted sanders are surprisingly versatile, especially if you choose a combination unit with both a belt and disc. Most have 6" × 48" belts, combined with a disc measuring 9" to 12" in diameter. Small models with 1" × 36" belts and 4" discs are also available and are great for sharpening, as well as sanding.

Open-End Drum Sanders
These sanders are a breed apart, useful for finishing — and doing mild flattening — of wide panels. They're not planers, but are low-cost substitutes for wide-belt production sanders that cost thousands of dollars. They can give a good finish to most woods, and make doing wide tables and countertops a simpler job.

Understanding Random Orbit Features

With a sustained orbital motion of the sanding pad, a random orbit sander (ROS) is very useful, removes material fairly quickly and offers a good finish. More powerful random orbit sanders rival a belt sander for taking off material, but they are easier to control and leave a finer finish. Plan on buying one; they're perfect for most tasks.

Orbit Size and Speed

Random orbit sanders offer swirls as small as ³⁄₃₂"; and the smaller, the better. The randomness of the orbits keeps swirl marks from forming. Pad speeds vary from 8,000 to 13,000 rpm. Some have a variable speed option set on a dial to suit the material and grit used.

Power

Don't look for humongous motors on any random orbit sander. You'll find they range from as little as 1.4 amps up to 5.5 amps in right-angle powerhouses.

Dust Control

Punched holes in the sanding pads lead into a small bag or hard cup for dust collection. Buy your paper with the same arrangement of holes as the sanding pad, or buy a punch and do your own hole-making. While the bag or cup will collect some dust, most aren't very efficient. For the best dust collection, hook the tool to a shop vacuum.

Pad Type

Pads use either adhesive-backed or hook-and-loop sandpaper discs; one company makes a pad that flips to accept either type. "Contour pads" are softer material to conform to uneven surfaces. Most also accept wool polishing pads and applicator pads for waxes, used with the soft contour pads.

Price

Expect to pay at least $50 for a small random orbit sander, up to over $100. For right-angle models (useful for very heavy material removal), prices begin at about $100 and go up to over $200.

Makita's random orbit sander, model BO5010, offers variable speed and efficient dust collection.

In Random Orbit Sanders, Look For:

- Convenient, comfortable operation.
- Size of pad, cost of sandpaper to fit, attachment method (adhesive or hook-and-loop?).
- Level of vibration.
- Variable- or single-speed?
- How many orbits per minute does it give you? More is better.
- What size are the orbits? Smaller is better.
- How long is the cord? At least 10' is best.
- Is the switch dust-protected? Sander switches need dust protection.

Understanding Detail and Contour Sander Features

Detail sanders are a recent innovation. The original triangle sander is still around, with many variations. This tool is superb for finish-sanding in areas such as window muntins, molding details and other hard-to-get-to spots, using one hand. Sanding speeds range from 9,000 orbits per minute (opm) to as high as 21,000 opm.

Contour sanders have bodies like detail sanders with shaped nosepieces that slip onto the tip of the sander, allowing you to get into tight corners, curves, veined work and similar spots. Models may come with as many as 17 different sanding profiles.

Sandpaper Choice

Contour and detail sanders use special paper, in rolls as wide as the nosepieces. Don't choose a model that requires sandpaper you can only get at one store.

Power and Speed

Contour and detail sanders offer single speeds — 6,000 strokes per minute (spm) — or variable speeds. Contour sanders typically operate at lower speeds than detail sanders. The motors are all small; none are over 2 amps.

Price

Detail sanders mostly cost well under $100, with plenty of good choices around $50. Most contour sanders run between $75 and $150.

In Detail and Contour Sanders, Look For:

- Level of vibration. Less is better.
- How easily do nosepieces (contour sanders) slide on and off when loaded with paper?
- Variable or single speed?
- Does it feel good in your hand overall?
- How many orbits per minute does it give you? More is better.
- What size are the orbits? Smaller is better.
- How long is the cord?

Bosch's belt sander, model
1274DVS, has a 3" x 21" belt size
with variable speed.

Porter-Cable's profile sander, model 9444VS, comes with 17
sanding profiles for a variety of intricate applications.

Understanding Belt Sander Features

Belt sanders are a major step up in power and material removal. They also help you quickly ruin wood, because a slight tilt in any direction can gouge out lots of wood in a hurry. These tools employ a belt with outward-facing grit that runs around a pair of wheels. A platen (a flat, metal supporting plate) between the two wheels provides a flat sanding surface. The sander has a tracking knob, and a quick-release lever for easy adjustment and change of the belts. Belts are driven either at single speed (up to 1,600 rpm), or variable. In general, these are not the tools of fine woodworking, but are invaluable in flattening a panel and other aggressive wood removal.

Belt Size

Standard sizes include 3" × 21", 3" × 24", 4" × 21" and 4" × 24". Belt grits are as coarse as 36, but only as smooth as 120. Belt sanders size and shape wood, bringing it to a semi-finished state.

Power

Smaller belt sanders need power, and you'll find motors from around 6 amps up to 12 amps. Lower-amp motors are for the 3" × 21" models. As belt size increases, power rises.

Weight

None of these sanders will be light. Weight is needed for motor power and machine durability. The lightest, highest-quality 3" × 21" belt sanders are about 8 pounds, with larger models climbing to over 12 pounds. Weight is less important than overall feel, fit and balance — which are all factors you will have to judge personally.

Dust collection

Dust is sucked into a tube located on top of the belt sander, although some belt sanders do not offer integral dust collection and are intended to be used in conjunction with sanding tables.

Price

Belt sanders run from about $75 for a decent 3" × 21" sander to over $200 for a 4" × 24" sander. Select the best you can afford in the size you want or need.

In Belt Sanders, Look For:

- Level of vibration.
- Variable or single-speed?
- What belt sander size? Larger is faster on wide panels, but takes more muscle to control on anything smaller.
- Does it feel good overall? The belt sander is one handheld power tool that needs to feel solid and easy to control. Do front and rear handles suit your style of working?
- Does the belt tracking control work easily?
- Does the belt release work smoothly?
- Does it have a flat top? It's easier to change paper with a flat top, though this is not an essential.
- What is the weight? Hefty is good, but clumsy due to bad balance is not. You won't find a good belt sander under eight pounds, but working with more than 12 pounds gets tiring fast.
- What kind of dust collection does it have? It'll still probably be only semi-adequate.

Understanding Oscillating Spindle Features

The oscillating spindle sander has recently become affordable for the small woodshop. Spindle sanders make sanding interior curves, small pieces and thin pieces a safer and easier operation. A spindle, set in the center of a small table, oscillates up and down as it spins. Rpm is usually around 200, while the up and down strokes are around 60 per minute. One model offers an oscillating belt sander that can be replaced with a spindle. Spindles are of rubber and accept sanding sleeves in a variety of grits. Spindle diameters are variable from ½" to 3", while spindle height depends on the brand, with most in the 4" to 4½" range.

Ridgid's oscillating edge belt/spindle sander, model number EB4424, with tilting table, offers the best of two worlds.

Power
Powered by light-duty induction motors, small 3½-amp motors work just fine.

Dust Collection
Available on most. Some machines come with dust collection ports or hoods, others with dust collection bags. Dust collection is necessary.

Price
Expect to pay at least $150 for an oscillating spindle sander. The combination belt-and-spindle sander sells for about $250.

In Oscillating Spindle Sanders, Look For:
- What is the table material? Most are composite or laminated wood — but cast iron is better, although it costs more.
- Do the inserts lift out easily?
- Do the rubber spindle covers change easily?
- Does it come with a full selection of spindles and inserts?

Understanding Stationary Belt/Disc Sander Features
The stationary belt/disc sander is a great tool for shaping and finish sanding larger objects. Typically, 6" × 48" abrasive belts are used with a cast-iron table. Most models also include a disc sander, with discs available in 9", 10" or 12" sizes. Fences make square sanding easy.

Stands
Most stationary sanders come with either closed or open stands, but a few models come with no stand at all, so keep this in mind when pricing the tools. Store-bought stands cost $70 and up. Stands give an overall height of about 36" to 44" with the sanding belt horizontal.

Weight
Weights range from 125 pounds (no stand) past 200 pounds for closed-base industrial use machines.

Power
The most common motor is a 1½-horsepower single-phase induction motor. Belt speeds are 1,500- to 2,000-feet per minute. Discs rotate at 2,500 rpm or so. (Anything more than that for the disc rotation pulls work from your hands, but speeds below 1800 rpm don't remove material fast enough.)

Belt Release
Many models offer a quick-release for the sanding belts. If there isn't one, expect to spend 15 minutes or more when you need to change belts.

Dust Collection
Dust collection ports are in various places depending on whether the bases are enclosed or not. Do not buy any new sander that doesn't have a dust collection port. The port should be located where it will draw directly from the underside of the belt and from the bottom edge of the disc.

Price
Good, hobby-shop belt/disc sanders, with 1-hp motors and open stands, sell for under $300. Heavier sanders without stands cost $450 to $700. For the small woodshop, expect to spend between $200 and $500.

In Stationary Belt/Disc Sanders, Look For:
- Easy-to-reach and operate controls? Tables remove, adjust and install easily? Belt removes, installs, adjusts with ease? This is important regardless of price.
- Well-machined, cast-iron tables.
- A belt speed of 1,500- to 2,000-feet per minute.
- Does the belt assembly elevate and lower easily?
- Is there a quick-release for the belt?

Understanding Open-End Drum Sander Features
Open-end drum sanders make the finishing of wide panels almost an easy job. They are not planers, removing only a small amount of wood with each pass, but can smooth pieces up to 3' wide. Abrasive strips wound around the drums sand the panels smooth as they're carried through the machine by a powered belt on the lower table. There aren't many on the market aimed at the home shop, so choices are limited.

Sizes

There are now several brands available at hobby shop prices. The 16" cantilever types, open on one end to allow two passes and doubling of capacity. Stands are usually extra with the 16" models, but are standard with the 18". Weight in all cases is under 200 pounds, and under 150 pounds with the smaller tools.

Price

Drum sanders start at about $500 and jump quickly to over $1,000.

In Open-End Drum Sanders, Look For:

- How wide is it? Wider is better.
- How easy is it to wind on and lock in place the abrasive strips? Is a special tool needed? If so, is it supplied?
- What are the feed speeds?
- What is the sanding drum speed(s)? A spread of at least 800 feet per minute is good.

The Coin Flip:

The random orbit sander is probably the most important sander in today's woodshop. Get one. You may end up wanting two, one right angle for heavy work plus a one-hand model for lighter finishing work.

Contour and detail sanders are nice to have and not very expensive. For anyone doing scroll-saw or other fine work, or working with muntins and detail carvings, they're life savers. Select the brand that feels the sturdiest to you, is most comfortable in your hand and has a price you like.

Belt sanders are optional. A random orbit sander may be a better answer; it allows for nearly-as-fast wood removal, is easier to control and yields a much finer finish. If you do decide you need a belt sander, then the 3" × 21" model may be your answer. For wider stock, the 4" × 21" and 4" × 24" sanders are better. Select the sander that feels best of all those that meet your needs.

Oscillating sanders are easy choices. They do just one thing, so they must do it well. Prices vary widely, but you can get a decent tool for under $200. For most of us, the less costly oscillating sanders do the job well and do it for years. If you feel a need for using an oscillating sander on flat surfaces, then find a machine that also offers an oscillating belt assembly. Make your selection based on individual machine features such as number of spindles, length of spindles and size of table.

Your belt/disc sander covers any need for sanding objects quickly, making sure surfaces are kept flat. If you need a fast, accurate final-shaping machine, give some thought to one of these sanders. Select for enough power and a large enough disc and belt. Effective dust collection is important, as is the ease of the belt change. Don't buy any machine that makes you disassemble things to change belts. Make sure there are two cast-iron tables (one each for the disc and belt) and that the belt table removes quickly and easily.

Drum sanders are handy machines, but they are easily knocked out of adjustment because of their cantilever construction. But for anyone doing lots of wide-board sanding or needing to surface lots of small pieces, drum sanders are the answer. They're safe, durable and easy to keep dust-free. But bear in mind that even the lowest-price unit is expensive.

Performax's open-end thickness sander from JET, model 22-44, will sand up to a 22"-wide board in one pass or a 44"-wide board by rotating the piece.

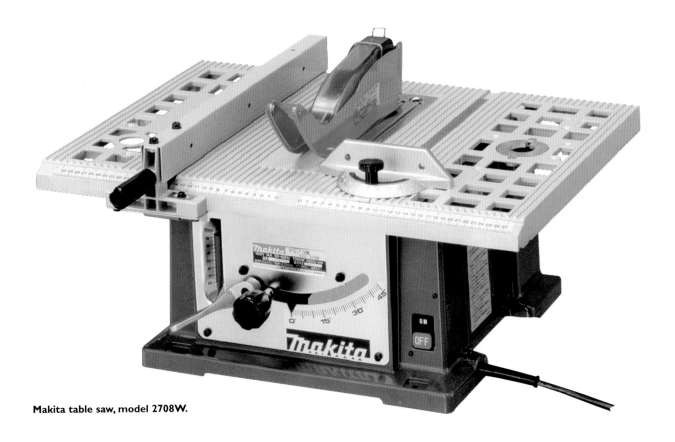

Makita table saw, model 2708W.

For most woodworkers, the table saw is the single-most important tool in your woodworking shop. It's the first thing you should buy and the tool that should command the lion's share of your budget. A good table saw — and we're about to tell you how to identify the good ones — will give you precise, square cuts. Precision, repeatability and ease of setup is what you're paying for.

If all this talk of money has you nervous, you can relax. A good table saw doesn't have to have a price tag that makes you sweat just adding up the digits.

And, truth be told, some woodworkers don't absolutely need a table saw. For example, is most of your woodworking centered around a lathe? Then you're probably better off maxing out your charge card on a really good lathe and band saw.

For the rest of us, though, a table saw is the working center of our shop. What other single tool lets us easily rip and crosscut soft and hardwoods, make dadoes, rabbets and tapered cuts, or even manufacture wood trim when used with a molding head? There isn't much a table saw can't do with the right combination of jigs and accessories.

In fact, if you prefer the quiet pleasures of hand tools, a table saw still makes sense as the one power tool you do own. You can easily get by with hand saws, hand planes and sanding blocks, but it's pretty hard to get straight, parallel second sides in your stock without a table saw.

What's Out There

As befits the most important tool in any woodshop, there's no shortage of table saws available. They come in three basic styles: benchtop, contractor's and cabinet. You can find something to suit just about any budget and any shop.

Before you spend even a minute shopping, learn what the significant differences are between these three types of table saws. You need to match up the saws' capabilities and liabilities if you're going to get the right saw for your situation.

Benchtop Table Saws

The benchtop table saw offers an affordable (and space-saving) option, especially for the casual user. Light weight and portability are two key advantages (from one perspective), but are also the main knocks against these saws.

The benchtop table saw is usually the least accurate, least powerful and least versatile saw you can buy. Just about any contractor's saw will leave the typical benchtop model choking in its sawdust. But if you lack the space or the budget for one of the bigger saws, then a benchtop model becomes a reasonable option. Some of the top-of-the-line benchtop models are quite competent.

Benchtop saws are usually the least expensive option, with plenty of OK choices under $300 — half what you'd pay for a used cabinet saw. A benchtop table saw also makes plenty of sense if its main use is for rough carpentry on home fix-up projects. Precision cutting just isn't as important in that type of situation.

Benchtop table saws come with either 8¼" or 10" blades. The high-end models will have rip fences approaching the precision found on some contractor's saws. Unfortunately, they can't make cuts to the same width and sometimes won't cut as deeply, regardless of their listed capacity. Benchtop saws, by their basic design, have the blade at-

tached directly to the motor; there are no belts as there are on larger saws. This reduces the depth-of-cut by a sometimes-significant fraction, though you might not realize it by reading ads or catalog copy. Universal motors are the rule with this type of saw, so you're going to deal with more noise and less power than you'd experience with the induction motors used in bigger saws.

Benchtop horsepower claims are largely irrelevant. Instead, check the motor amperage, because more amps equals more power.

What you really want to pay attention to and measure for yourself, is the depth-of-cut and maximum rip cut. The maximum rip cuts in low-cost saws may be only about 9¼", while better benchtops may offer maximum rips of 24" to 30". If you never rip anything but solid wood boards, then 9¼" may be sufficiently wide, but, for most woodworkers, it's too limiting.

A good rip fence is a necessity for any table saw, and especially so with a benchtop. This is one area where manufacturers often try to save a few bucks. If the fence is lightweight and flexible, it'll be unstable. If it doesn't lock tight and hold its position parallel

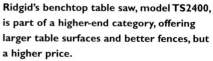

Ridgid's benchtop table saw, model TS2400, is part of a higher-end category, offering larger table surfaces and better fences, but a higher price.

BLADES

There are three primary types of table saw blades. The rip blade is the most useful. The combination blade works for most jobs, though it's not suitable for extensive ripping. The cut-off blade does a superb job of giving smooth cut-offs in most materials.

Table saw blades of decent quality range in price from $30 to over $100 (in 10" size). At prices like that, it helps to ask your woodworking friends what they've found that works. If there's no one to ask, select a name brand blade that has a mid-range price. Use it long enough to get thoroughly familiar with your saw. At that point, you may want to move sideways, up, or down (unlikely) in your blade choices. To start with, choose one rip blade and one cut-off blade. Experiment with combination blades at a later date.

Tip *One way to get a benchtop saw performing better, especially when cutting thick, wet or hard wood, is to use either a smaller-diameter blade or a thin kerf blade. The motor won't have to work as hard to spin the smaller (or thinner) blade and your cutting should go quicker. Just make sure it's a high-quality blade.*

to the blade, accurate cuts are just plain impossible. If you purchase a contractor's saw with a junky rip fence, you can use the thing for a door prop, and buy a good after-market fence. But benchtop table saws don't readily accept auxiliary fences, so the factory-supplied offering needs to be of some quality.

Fences are easy to check in the store. Set the fence, then push against the middle and the back of the fence to see if it holds tight. Bring along a buddy to keep the saw from sliding around and to protect you from any alarmed salespeople.

Here's a second test for quality in benchtop table saws: Making sure the saw is unplugged, run the blade all the way up. Grip the blade and twist your hand (wear a glove or put a rag around

the blade). If the blade twists, then the arbor and motor mounts have too much "give" in them and you won't be able to make accurate cuts, no matter how good everything else might be.

Dust collection efficiency varies widely with small table saws. Some make little or no provision for dust collection, while others have 2-inch-diameter ports ready for hookup. If you don't care about dust collection — and you should — at least invest in some quality dust masks.

Pricing Benchtop Saws

There are some good, quality benchtop table saws out there, and a lot more inadequate saws. The good ones will cost nearly $500; the not-so-good less than $150. In between those two price points, you'll find a lot of saws, at a wide variety of quality levels. As always, keep a close eye on sales and rebate offers. Since there is a lot of competition in this market segment, you should expect to see some good deals.

In Benchtop Table Saws, Look For:

- Clean castings and sheet-metal in table and housing. Some benchtop

saws use plastic bodies to reduce weight and cost. That can be good or bad, depending on how well-made the saw is. A flexible saw is an inaccurate saw.

- Ease of movement when setting blade height and blade angles, plus solid lockdowns to hold the settings.
- A good fence that sets up easily parallel to the blade and locks down tight.
- Is it stable when on a flat surface?
- How large is the main-adjustment wheel? Larger is better.
- Do you like the way it feels? Are the controls where you think they should be? (Try 'em!)
- What's the motor amperage? Fifteen amps is better than 13.
- How thick is the table insert and how does it lock in place? This affects both the durability of the stock insert and the ease of making custom inserts. Thicker is usually better. Can you get your hand into the opening so you can change blades? Better check.
- Weight? Lighter is better if portability and easy storage are concerns.
- How do the warranty, price and brand stack up?

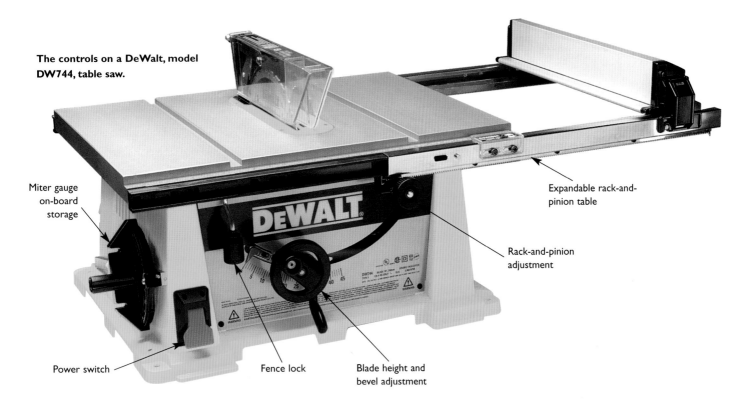

The controls on a DeWalt, model DW744, table saw.

Miter gauge on-board storage

Expandable rack-and-pinion table

Rack-and-pinion adjustment

Power switch

Fence lock

Blade height and bevel adjustment

JET contractor's table saw, model JWTS-10CW2 PFX, offers near-professional performance with 52" fence capacity, high-quality precision rip fence and solid cast-steel wings.

Contractor's Table Saws

The contractor's table saw is a workhorse that doesn't expect to be pampered. It's a solid step up from the benchtop saw, and is probably a good choice for most shops. The contractor's table saw combines limited portability — at around 200 pounds, these things aren't lightweights — stability and enough power to produce good, clean, accurate cuts in hardwoods. They've usually got enough "oomph" to let you work fast, too.

The basic contractor's saw will probably come with a stand (and the motor usually hanging out the back) with a single belt running to an arbor located under the table. Expect the induction motor to run from 12 to 18 amps, and be rated at 1½ to 2 horsepower. That's real, delivered horsepower, not ad claims. Much more than 2 hp puts too much strain on the single-belt/pulley power transmission system.

The arbor runs in ball bearings and is mounted under the table. The sturdier that mount, the longer the bearings will last and the more accurate the saw will be over time. The table itself is (or should be, if woodworking is your main focus) of cast iron. Side extensions may be cast iron, aluminum or sheet metal. Some models will have one cast-iron table extension and the other table, usually the right, will be laminate-covered particleboard or MDF. This allows for special rip fences of great length (up to about 52") without adding an insane weight load. This same method for extension tables is used on cabinet saws, as well.

Actual positioning of adjustment wheels doesn't vary a lot, but the size and weight of the wheels make a difference in how easily the saw adjusts, as does the number of revolutions needed to bring the blade to the correct height. Some saws require about 25 revolutions to move from its highest to its lowest height, while a few require up to 40. The number of turns is a trade-off, since fewer revolutions means each one requires a bit more energy, but a larger number of revolutions means setting up the saw is more time consuming.

The blade guard on a contractor's saw mounts at the rear of the blade, and is connected through the table insert. These inserts are heftier and wider than what you'll find on benchtop saws. They're also easier to replace

DADO HEADS

Dado heads cut dadoes, or grooves, in wood. They are extremely important in most woodworking shops for cabinet and shelving construction. They're major time savers and you probably need one. There are three types of dado heads: the single-blade wobble type, the dual-blade wobble type and the stacked dado.

Generally, the single-blade wobble type is the least desirable and the least durable, but it's also the least expensive. The single blade moves from side to side in the groove, but in its movement, it leaves a central upside down "V" or "U" that has to be removed with a chisel.

The double-blade wobble leaves a cleaner bottom, but is as costly (or even more so) than a stacked dado set.

The stacked dado set consists of two outside blades and a variable number of inner blades that can be assembled to cut a wide range of groove widths. It's the preferred standard for dado work.

Single-blade wobble dado cutters are available for as little as $40, while the dual blade and stack units start in the $90 range and go up to about $200.

top saws. They're also easier to replace with optional or shop-built zero-clearance, dado and molding inserts, because the material is thicker, lending itself to easier reproduction in plastic, wood or metal. The insert may be held down with a screw, or it could be a snap-in type, usually held with a small spring steel strip that fits under a lip at the back of the insert's hole.

A good contractor's saw will have at least 10¾" of table in front of the blade slot and 11" in front of a fully raised blade. More is better.

The motor suspended from the rear of the typical contractor's saw makes dust collection more difficult. Many of today's saws can be ordered with a plastic dust-collection plate that fits underneath the cabinet. It's a start, but dust collection will never be as good as with a cabinet saw.

Contractor's saws accept the full array of accessory rip fences, and if you're buying the saw new, the supplied fence can be quite good. Their tables are the standard 27" deep that's necessary to fit an after-market fence. In fact, you'll find plenty of real Beisemeyer fences as well as Beisemeyer clones available, as either a standard item or as an option. Changeover from a low-cost manufacturer's fence to a top-grade accessory fence is one of the most practical, easiest and useful upgrades. Many companies offer a choice of two or more fences other than the basic model. Yes, the extra quality fence is worth it, even though sometimes it may be half the cost of the table saw itself. In some cases, it's now possible to buy an excellent manufacturer's fence without having to spend extra money — definitely the way to go.

What To Pay

Depending on the fence and other accessories (extension tables, legs, etc.), a basic 10" contractor's saw with a stand may be as low as $400. A complete package of saw, good fence, wider table and other features will be around $850.

In Contractor's Table Saws, Look For:

- Clean metal castings. The lack of attention here is usually reflected in the price, and it's not one of those things you can fix yourself.
- Ease of movement of blade vertically and when setting angles. Do they lock down tight when set?
- Are the hand wheels easy to reach and move?
- Does the fence set easily and lock solidly, parallel to the blade, and give you the impression it will deliver repeatable accuracy?
- Overall good fit and finish.
- Are the wings sheet-metal or cast iron? Cast iron is better.
- Are the cast-iron wings open or solid? Solid is better.
- How large is the main-adjustment wheel? Larger is better. Most are around 5".
- Are the controls easy for you to reach?
- Can the motor be converted from 110 volts to 220 volts? Is it at least 12 amps?
- How thick is the table insert? This bears on both the durability of the supplied insert and the ease of making custom inserts. Thicker is better.
- Weight? Heavier is better. No contractors saw should weigh under 200 pounds.
- How does it stack up to others in warranty and price?

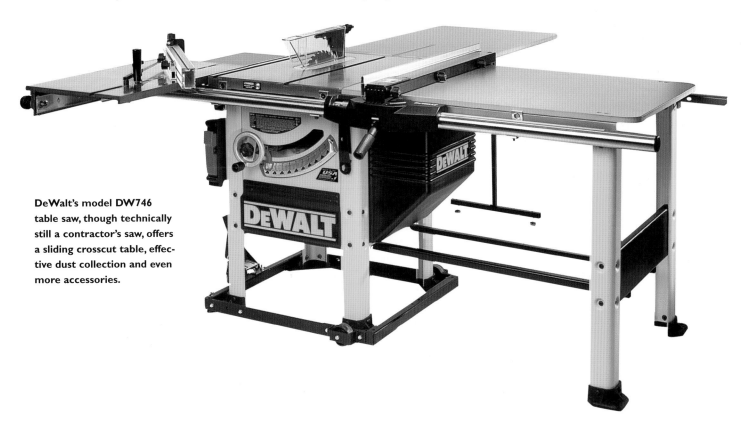

DeWalt's model DW746 table saw, though technically still a contractor's saw, offers a sliding crosscut table, effective dust collection and even more accessories.

Cabinet Saws

Sometimes called "production saws," cabinet saws fill the lottery-winning dreams of plenty of woodworkers. And why not? You get more power in what's usually a smaller footprint than with a contractor's saw, plus greater weight that helps absorb vibration. Cabinet saws are quieter, more powerful, offer every feature possible and announce to your woodworking buddies that you've officially "arrived."

The cabinet saw in its most basic form has a cast iron top with a sheet-metal cabinet (hence the name) that encloses the motor, the arbor and all the workings. The basic motor is a 3-hp unit, designed to work on only 220 volts. Trunnions for table adjustments are twice the size and weight of those in a contractor's saw, while adjustment wheels are also heavier and larger in diameter.

The cabinet saw is designed to earn its keep by working all day at cutting 2" thick and thicker (8/4 and up) hardwood such as oak and walnut. It's a distinct pleasure to change from a lighter saw that was stuttering when cutting heavy stock, to the power of a cabinet saw that easily slices through the same stubborn wood.

Table extensions are solid cast iron, though the right-side extension is eliminated if a rip fence with long bars is added. Rip fences available for cabinet saws are of similar design as those available for contractor's saws, though often of larger height and width. Manufacturers usually give you a choice of a basic rip fence and one or two or more higher cost and better fence options. Though most dealers and catalogs don't mention it, if you're trading up and already have a superb fence that you want to keep on using, you can order the cabinet saw (and most contractor's saws for that matter) without a fence.

Because a cabinet saw totally encloses the motor, it must be a fan-cooled type or it will burn up quickly.

Delta's model 36820 Unisaw, in many incarnations, has been the standard cabinet saw for home woodworkers for decades.

The standard motor is typically a 3-hp unit, but single-phase, 5-hp motors are available for those with really heavy-duty cutting plans. Power transmission is via multiple V-belts, producing greater efficiency because there's less slippage.

The cabinet saw's table should not only have solid extensions, but be thicker than the table on a contractor's saw. The fit and finish should be at least as good as that on a premium-priced contractor's saw, with the table nicely milled to a fine, smooth surface.

Miter gauges run in T-slots cut in the table, which means the gauge isn't going to drop out as you get to its full reach. Inserts will be heavier because they're a little larger, and usually thicker than those on a contractor's saw. Expect the inserts to be drop-in types, with Allen screws in each corner to level it with the tabletop. Because of their thickness (most are about ⅜" to ½"), it's simple to find material to make your own zero clearance and dado inserts.

You'll find at least 11¼" of table real estate in front of a fully raised blade on these saws. Combine the table depth with the T-slot miter gauge, and you get a cut-off depth of at least 15".

All of this extra metal on the saw adds up. Cabinet saws' weights start at about 350 pounds and go up to over 500 pounds. If the fence and its bars are included, even more weight is added to your shipping charges. The cabinet saw is a tool that demands either a helper or special arrangements with the trucking company to unload. They're distinctly unpleasant to wrestle around if you're alone.

Most hobbyist woodworkers will stop with the basic 10" cabinet saw, a perfectly adequate size. However, you can get heavier and even more expensive 12" and 14" versions if you feel a need for even more power and speed.

The cabinets have various access doors and ports. There may be a front door, a handy device for reaching in to find dropped arbor nuts and table inserts. There should be a side door covering the motor, and below this will be the ducting for a dust collector or at least space for one after you get tired of constantly having to sweep up the massive amounts of sawdust these saws produce.

What You'll Pay

If a cabinet saw is what you must have, the price to get in the game starts around $750 and can climb well past $2000. Look for sales and rebates because competition is fierce and you should use it to your advantage. Some manufacturers are now building a lot of value into their lower-priced cabinet saws, so definitely shop around. And remember when comparing prices to include any shipping charges, as they can vary widely.

In Cabinet Saws, Look For:

- Clean castings: Any lack of perfection here is often reflected in the price.
- Clean, accurate milling of the tabletop.
- Ease of vertical movement of the blade is important.
- How large and comfortable are the adjustment wheels? Larger is better.
- Does the angle adjustment wheel move easily?
- Are the hand wheels easy to reach and do they lock down solidly?
- Does the fence have good, repeatable accuracy?
- Does the fence lock solidly?
- What's the quality of the miter gauge? Some manufacturers throw junky miter gauges onto expensive saws.
- How thick is the top? Thicker is better.
- Does it have a magnetic on/off switch?
- Are the controls easy for you to reach? Most switches can be moved from left to right, but a few can't without major drilling.
- What is the horsepower of the motor? Single-phase motors for these saws runs from 2 to 5 hp.
- Does the saw come with a blade? Most don't, surprisingly, when you look at the price tag, or come with a nearly useless blade.
- How thick is the table insert? This bears on both the durability of the stock insert and the ease of making custom inserts. Thicker is better.
- Weight? Heavier is better. No cabinet saw should weigh under 350 pounds.

Understanding the Features

Biesemeyer Fence System

The standard in after-market accessory fences, the actual design is available from a number of manufacturers. Some saws will come with this fence as standard equipment. Other manufacturers offer variations plus additional features and will have their own unique name for their version of this fence. Note that small benchtop saws cannot accept these accessory fences.

Thermal Overload Switch

This is a switch that prevents the motor from overheating under heavy use. A reset switch gets you back to work once things have cooled off.

Table Insert

Also called the throat plate, it covers the opening in the saw table where the blade rides. You remove it to change blades.

Magnetic Start Switch

A type of switch that turns the saw off if the power fails for any reason, and stays off until you push the button again. Often standard equipment on cabinet saws, this is a worthwhile safety feature. Magnetic switches can easily be added to any saw or other stationary power tool. Most, but not all, magnetic switches also incorporate thermal overload protection.

Link Belt

An optional type of drive belt for belt-driven tools. Link belts reduce noise and vibration compared to standard rubber V-belts, because they're more flexible. Usually sold by the foot. A worthwhile option which improves the performance of almost any contractor's saw.

The Coin Flip:

If at all possible, buy at least a good contractor's saw. These workhorses are more than acceptable for most woodworking, providing a great combination of power, features and cost. Over the last few years, the manufacturers have metamorphosed them from construction-site tools into tools more suited for

FENCES

Fences are the key element of a table saw's accuracy. You can have the most perfectly machined saw table, silky smooth power transmission, a mirror-like finish, diamond-encrusted saw blades, and none of it is worth a stitch if your fence won't do the job.

T-square fences based on the Biesemeyer pattern are the most popular. These fences install easily on contractor and cabinet saws, set up easily, lock solidly and may outlast the saw.

Other fence types involve round fence bars and strong Allen screws, or various types of locking assemblies. There are a wide number of worthwhile models out there, the worst of which is better than most of the standard fences supplied with the saw. They should be priced from about $200 to $400.

The smaller your table-saw shopping budget, the more it should be devoted to the best fence/saw combination you can find.

serious woodworking. Get at least 1½ hp, enough for reasonably heavy work, and solidly built so it holds its accuracy over time. For most small woodworking shops, there's no need for anything more.

For the smallest shops, very occasional use or a very tight budget, a benchtop saw may be the answer. Though the more expensive benchtop saws are better saws, the price puts you in the entry-level-contractor's-saw hierarchy. Choose wisely.

Every woodworker dreams of owning a full-fledged cabinet saw; you won't get many arguments as to their desirability and worth. Ask yourself, however, whether this is a case of "need" or "want." Cabinet saws deliver from 3 to 5 hp, with enough extension-table real estate on tap to land a small aircraft. But you'll also need 220-volt wiring in your shop, plenty of working room and up to $2,000 (with a few exceptions) for a proper setup with all the accessories. And you could spend even more than that.

All it Takes is
Money

So you're flipping through the newspaper and remember to check the lottery numbers to see how you did last night. Before you can scream "Norm Abrams!" you discover you're a millionaire. Congratulations. And you can now buy all the woodworking tools you've ever wanted. You start dreaming of that Delta Unisaw and that Porter-Cable 690 router set you've been drooling over. Wait a second, you can buy dozens of Unisaws. Don't stop there, what's the most expensive woodworking tools you can buy? Okay, splash some water on your face. While you haven't hit the lottery, let's do a little dreaming and see what $1,000,000 can buy (I love seeing that many zeros). We took each tool category in this book and chose the most amazing tool available in each category – money no object. Hope you enjoy the fantasy.

Makita's model LS711DWBEK 71/2" cordless slide compound miter saw has an 18-volt nickel-metal hydride battery, $529.

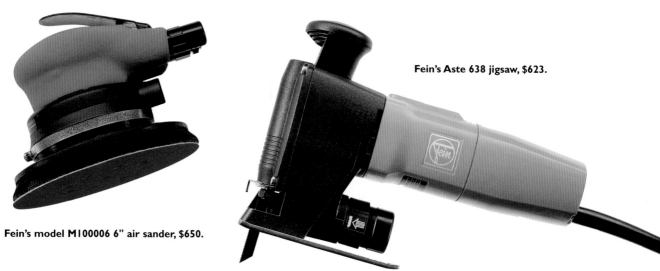

Fein's Aste 638 jigsaw, $623.

Fein's model M100006 6" air sander, $650.

Metabo's model BEAT214/2 R+L, 14.4-volt cordless drill, $437.

Lamello's Top 20 biscuit joiner, $679.

belt sander, 3" x 24", 9 amp, in-line, $445.

Laguna's model J-20 6.6-hp, 220-volt, three-phase jointer, $9,995.

Emglo's model W5B-80 compressor with 5-hp, 80-gallon tank, 23-amp and 230-volt with a max psi of 175, $2,420.

Bosch's model 1617EVS 3¼-hp router, $578.

Laguna's model P24 12" x 24" 5.5-hp thickness planer, $14,995.

Laguna's LT 18 RM 18" band saw, $3,295.

Senco's SLP20 finish nailer with 1" to 1⅝"
18-gauge brads, $195.

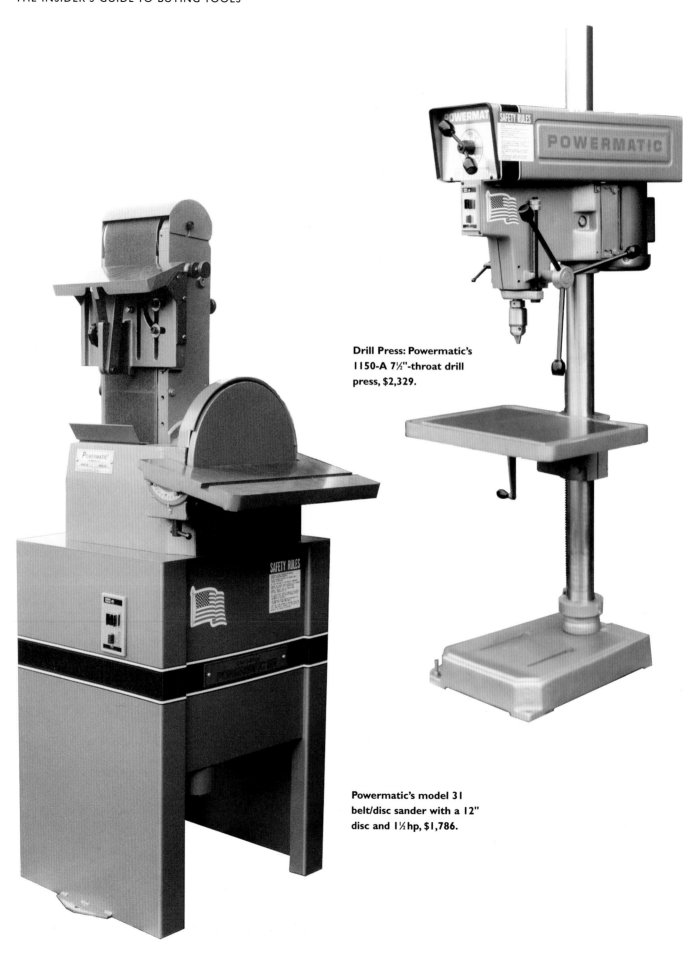

**Drill Press: Powermatic's
1150-A 7½"-throat drill
press, $2,329.**

**Powermatic's model 31
belt/disc sander with a 12"
disc and 1½ hp, $1,786.**

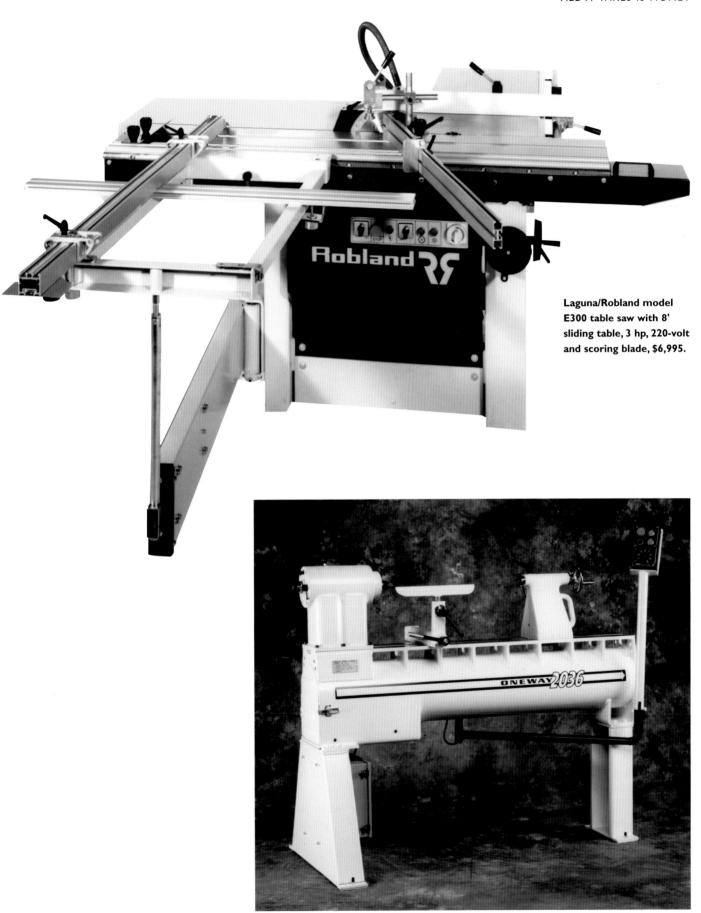

Laguna/Robland model
E300 table saw with 8'
sliding table, 3 hp, 220-volt
and scoring blade, $6,995.

Oneway's model 2036 floor-model lathe, 20" x 36" (20" swing above the bed and 36"-long
bed) and 1½ hp, $4,299.

All-in-ones

When someone says "combination tool," most Americans think of Shopsmith. While Shopsmith's machines are certainly combination tools, the more common use of combination tools occurs in Europe. One of the most common fixtures in European shops, the combination machine merges from two to five basic woodworking machines in a single machine ... making great use of limited workshop space. Even more valuable than that is the fact that many of these machines offer built-in capacity levels that are only available on very high-priced, stand-alone machines — such as a 12" jointer.

Though still tricky to find in the U.S., European-style combination machines are available as a tablesaw/shaper combination, a jointer/planer combination with an optional horizontal mortiser and as a combination of the first two — offering a tablesaw, shaper, jointer, planer, and (still optional) a horizontal mortiser. These five-function, (or five-in-ones) are available in a wide range of sizes, ranging from $1,000 to $15,000.

The combination machine that Americans are more familiar with (the Shopsmith-style machine), offers a table saw, drill press, lathe, horizontal boring machine and grinding wheel. A little different from the European version, these machines cost around $2,000.

The best way to determine if a com-

The Shopsmith Mark V.

bination machine makes sense for you is, first, determine which machines you need (i.e., do you really need a horizontal mortiser?) and then figure out what you would pay for those individual machines. If you already have a jointer, deduct that from the overall cost. Chances are good that when you compare possible capacities to dollars, the combination machine will look like a pretty good deal. But, there are some trade-offs. Combination machines require transition time between operations, and to maximize their use you

will have to think more about ordering your work before changing the machine setup. Depending on the model, you may also find that even though you gain an 8" jointer, the bed or fence length is shorter than on a stand-alone machine.

Once you've done that math, go back to the other strong positive for combination machines — saving space. These machines aren't for everyone, but if they meet your requirements, your budget and your patience, they can be a good deal.

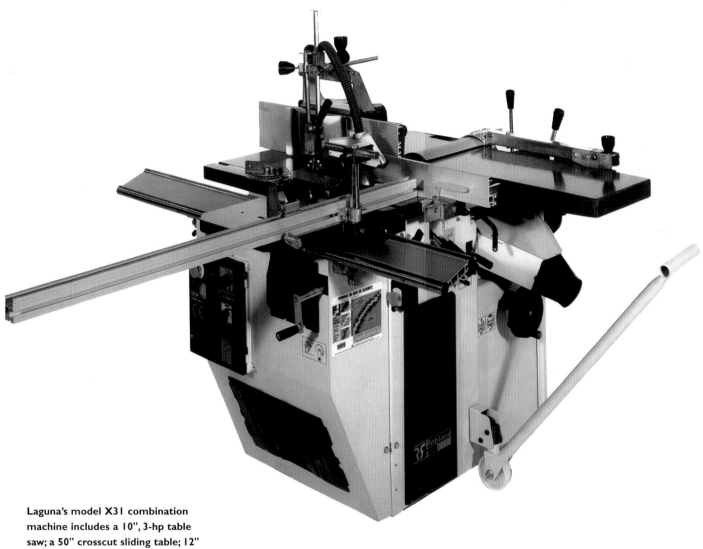

Laguna's model **X31** combination machine includes a 10", 3-hp table saw; a 50" crosscut sliding table; 12" jointer; 12" planer; 3-hp reversible shaper; slot mortiser and horizontal boring machine.

Buying Used

The main focus of this book is to educate you about making informed purchases of new woodworking power tools, but we would be remiss if we didn't discuss some of the great deals that are available by purchasing used tools. And we would be just as remiss if we didn't talk about the pitfalls.

Used tools can be purchased from a number of places: garage sales, flea markets and estate sales. If you're looking for larger equipment, many dealers and manufacturer's stores handle used or reconditioned tools. In general, used tools can be a bargain. But you can put a lot of effort into finding that bargain. If you make a career out of finding great deals on tools, then you're a collector, not a woodworker.

Power tools, such as drills, routers and jigsaws, can be a great bargain. But before you start shopping for one of these tools, check out what they cost new. Then set your limit for what price is a bargain, and how much time it's worth. Garage sales and reconditioned tools are going to be your best bets. In general these used tools are for sale for three reasons: someone bought a tool they didn't really need; someone is upgrading to a better tool; or there's something wrong with the tool. Beware of number three. Don't buy the tool without the chance to plug it in. Know enough about the tool to recognize if the brushes sound worn, if the chuck is frozen, if gears are stripped and, as simple as it may sound, if all the pieces

are there. If you buy a jigsaw at a great price, but the blade holding screw is missing, you may spend more time and money making the tool work than it's worth.

Larger tools, such as miter saws, band saws or table saws are a much larger investment. Again, some garage sales will turn up a good deal, but you're much better off checking newspaper ads in you area. Again, find out why the tool's for sale. If it's an upgrade, ask them why. You don't want to buy a tool that they found deficient even if it works. For serious purchases,

don't overlook a reputable machine dealer in your area. When a serious hobbyist decides it's time for a more serious tool, he may make a deal with his tool dealer to trade-in his old saw. This works well for the dealer and, in turn, can offer you some nice deals. If you aren't working through a retailer, you need to check some things yourself. Again, ask to see the machine run.

Check for obvious abuse, missing parts or excessive wear. If it's a planer or jointer, check the blades. They can be expensive to replace if they're damaged. Work the moveable parts on all

machinery. Check the tables for flatness and jointer tables for parallel. There's lots to look at, but don't be afraid to take as much time as you need ... it's your money.

With all that said, a new method of buying used tools is growing in popularity every day ... the Internet. When buying used tools essentially over the phone, you may get a chance to see photos of the tool and get someone's word about the condition. Some tools are worth the risk. Know what it would cost to fix if the tool isn't as described, and if parts are still available. You'll also have to factor in shipping, or time and effort to go to pick the tool up.

Some sites are dedicated to selling used tools, and a certain amount of trust has been developed in these sites. As the medium matures, it may be easier to buy on-line without concern, but use your head for now.

As a rule of thumb, a used tool is a good deal if you can save more than 25 percent over normal retail prices. Any less than that and your savings aren't as significant when weighed against a loss of warranty, unknown use and abuse to a tool and often settling for a tool that wasn't your first choice, merely because it's a deal.

Sources

Accuset
888-222-8144
www.accuset.com

Airy
562-926-6192
www.airytools.com

Belsaw
800-468-4449
www.belsaw.com

Black & Decker
800-544-6986
www.blackanddecker.com

Bosch – S-B Power Tools
877-267-2499
www.boschtools.com

Bridgewood – Wilke Machinery
800-235-2100
www.wilkemach.com

Campbell Hausfeld
800-543-6400
www.campbellhausfeld.com

Carba-Tec – Craft Supplies USA
800-551-8876
www.craftusa.com

Coleman Powermate
800-445-1805
www.nbmc.com/coleman

Craftsman – Sears
800-377-7414
www.sears.com/craftsman

Delta International Machinery
800-438-2486
www.deltawoodworking.com

DeVilbiss Air Power
800-888-2468
www.devap.com

DeWalt
800-433-9258
www.dewalt.com

Dremel
800-437-3635
www.dremel.com

Duo-Fast
888-386-3278
www.duo-fast.com

Dynabrade
800-828-7333
www.dynabrade.com

Emglo – Air-Mate/Airstream
814-269-1000

Excalibur – Sommerville Group
800-357-4118
www.tools-plus.com/toolsplus/exc.html

Fein Power Tools
800-441-9878
www.fein.com

Festo – Toolguide
888-463-3786
www.toolguide.net

Freud USA
800-334-4107
www.right-tool.com

General International
819-472-1161
www.general.ca/an/index2.htm

Grizzly International
800-523-4777
www.grizzlyindustrial.com

Hartville Tool
800-345-2396
www.hartvilletool.com

Hegner – Advanced Machinery
800-220-4264
www.advmachinery.com

Hitachi Power Tools
800-706-7337
www.hitachi.com

Inca – Garrett Wade
800-221-2942
www.garrettwade.com

Ingersoll Rand – Aro Tools
615-672-0321
www.ingersoll-rand.com

JET Equipment & Tools
800-274-6848
www.jettools.com

Laguna Tools
800-332-4094
www.lagunatools.com

Lamello – Colonial Saw
800-252-6355
www.csaw.com

Lobo Machine Power Tools
800-786-5626
www.lobomachine.com

Makita
800-462-5482
www.makita.com

Metabo
800-638-2264
www.metabousa.com

Milwaukee Tool
262-781-3600
www.mil-electric-tool.com

Mini Max SCM Group USA
800-292-1850
www.minimax-usa.com

Murphy-Rogers
323-587-4118

MVM Lathe – Colonial Saw
888-777-2729

North State – Leneave Machinery
800-442-2302

Oneway Manufacturing
800-565-7288

Panasonic Power Tools
800-338-0552
www.panasonic.com

Paslode
800-682-3428
www.paslode.com

Penn State Industries
800-377-7297
www.pennstateind.com

Porter-Cable
800-487-8665
www.porter-cable.com

Powermatic
800-248-0144
www.powermatic.com

Pro-Tech Power
800-888-6603

PS Wood – PS Machinery
800-939-4414

RBI Industries
800-487-2623
www.rbiwoodtools.com

Record Tools
800-268-0932

Reliant – Trendlines
800-877-7899
www.trend-lines.com

Ridgid – Emerson Tool
800-474-3443
www.ridgidwoodworking.com

Robland – Laguna Tools
800-332-4094
www.lagunatools.com

Ryobi Power Tools
800-323-4615
www.ryobi.com

Seco Machinery Tool
888-558-4628
www.seco-usa.com

Senco Products
888-222-8144
www.senco.com

Shopsmith
800-543-7586
www.shopsmith.com

Sioux Tools
800-722-7290

Skil – S-B Power Tools
877-SKIL 999
www.skiltools.com

Stanley Bostitch
800-556-6696
http://ec1.StanleyWorks.com

Star Tools
888-678-8777
www.411web.com/s/startools

Sunhill Machinery
800-929-4321
www.sunhillnic.com

Tradesman – Power Tool Specialists
800-243-5114
www.tradesman-rexon.com

Transpower – C.P. Tools
800-654-7702
www.cptools.com

VB36 Lathe – Craft Supplies
800-551-8876

Vega Enterprises
800-222-8342

Vicmarc – Craft Supplies
800-551-8876

Virutex – TNT-Virutex
800-868-9663

Wagner Electronic Products
800-727-4023
www.wwwagner.com

Williams & Hussey Machine
800-258-1380

Woodfast – Craft Supply
800-551-8876

Woodtek – Woodworker's Supply
800-645-9292

Index